The Blessing

ALSO BY GREGORY ORR

POETRY

The Caged Owl: New and Selected Poems
Orpheus and Eurydice
City of Salt
New and Selected Poems
We Must Make a Kingdom of It
The Red House
Gathering the Bones Together
Burning the Empty Nests

CRITICISM

Poetry As Survival
Poets Teaching Poets: Self and the World,
edited with Ellen Bryant Voigt
Richer Entanglements: Essays and Notes on Poetry and Poems
Stanley Kunitz: An Introduction to the Poetry

The Blessing

A Memoir

GREGORY ORR

Council Oak Books
San Francisco / Tulsa

Some names and identifying details have been changed in this autobiographical narrative in order to protect the privacy of individuals.

Council Oak Books, LLC
1290 Chestnut Street, Ste. 2, San Francisco, CA 94109
1615 S. Baltimore Avenue, Ste. 3, Tulsa, OK 74119
THE BLESSING: *A Memoir.* Copyright © 2002 by Gregory Orr.

ISBN 1-57178-111-0
First edition / First printing.
Printed in Canada.
02 03 04 05 06 07   5 4 3 2 1

For Trisha, who believed in this book

Many people read this book as it struggled toward this form and gave me the benefits of their generous responses. Among them: Deborah Eisenberg, David Wyatt, David Gates, David and Joan Grubin, Don Hall, Howard Norman, Jonathan and Alice Orr, Ann Beattie, Mary Oliver, Staige Blackford, and Molly Cook. In particular I would like to thank my wife, Trisha Orr, who inspired the project and gave encouragement at every stage; Andrew Blauner, my agent, whose faith in this book exceeded my own at crucial moments; and Kevin Bentley, my editor, whose genial confidence was essential; Paulette Millichap, Ja-lene Clark, and Carol Haralson whose hard work and goodwill brought this book into the world.

Yes

Burden and blessing—
two blossoms
on the same branch.

To be so lost
in this radiant wilderness.

Contents

Part Four

Part One

Part One

1

Blessing

DO I DARE TO SAY MY BROTHER'S DEATH WAS A BLESSING? Who would recoil first from such a statement? A reader, unsure of its context, but instinctively uneasy with the sentiment? Or me, who knows more of the context than I sometimes think I can bear, having spent most of my life struggling with that death because I caused it? Can I keep my own nerve long enough to work my way through the strangeness of that word?

In French, the verb *blesser* means "to wound." In English, "to bless" is to confer spiritual power on someone or something by words or gestures. When children are christened or baptized in some Christian churches, the priest or minister blesses them by sprinkling holy water on their faces. But the modern word has darker, stranger roots. It comes from the Old English *bletsian* which meant "to sprinkle with blood" and makes me think of ancient, grim forms of religious sacrifice where blood not water was the liquid possessing supernatural power—makes me remember standing as a boy so close to a scene of violence that the blood of it baptized me.

To wound, to confer spiritual power, to sprinkle with blood. There is something about the intersection of these three meanings that penetrates to the heart of certain violent events of my childhood. I feel as if life itself were trying to reveal some mystery to me by making those three sources meet in my own life.

To wound. To cause blood to flow out of a mortal body. To stand so near that I was spattered with the blood of it. And yet I did not die. *Why was I spared?* Now that I am in my fifties, I am finally brave enough to ask that aloud, although it is a question that has moved like an underground river below my whole life since that day, moved there with the steady, insistent rhythm of a heartbeat, as if the words themselves made the earth pulse through my feet.

Why was I spared? I'm not sure there is any answer to my question. I know I don't expect the answer to come from anyone else. I don't even expect it to come from me. Maybe it's because I'm a poet and I've spent my adult life believing words have the power to reveal what is hidden, but I believe the answer to my question emerges from this odd word itself, this "blessing" that conceals within its history such terrible words as "wound" and "blood."

2

Guns

THERE WAS A RIDGE ABOVE THE FIELD. IT HAD BEEN CUT clear of trees when a power line went through the year before and now its shrub-grown flank sloped down sharply into the flat grassy field below. It was land we owned, part of the hundred acres of woods and fields that went with the old house my parents had bought two years back. It was Saturday, and we were digging a trench there, with shovels and a pick—my older brother, Bill, and me. It had the rough shape of something sextons might dig in a cemetery, but not nearly so deep. I was a skinny kid and tired easily. Whenever I stopped to catch my breath, I tried to adopt what seemed to me an adult's pose, resting my chin on my gloved hands folded over the top of the shovel handle and gazing casually out over the field as if there were something there to see, while my heart thumped against the wood handle and my open-mouthed panting made little, spasmodic breath-clouds that held briefly in the still November air.

Late that afternoon, back from his house calls and not yet due for evening hours in the office at the back of our house, Dad trudged up the hill to survey our progress. What he thought meant everything to us, and though it was a job anyone could do, we worried that somehow the trench we'd dug wasn't good enough. When he climbed down in it, the top hardly came above his shins, and it was too narrow for him to squat without banging his knees. "You'll have to do better than that," he said, brushing the dirt from his khaki pants.

Monday would be the first day of deer season. Long before dawn, we three would be crouched there in that same dank trench, each of us holding his own rifle. Bill was fourteen and had a .222; I was twelve and had been given a lightweight .22 for my eleventh birthday. Dad had a 30.06 whose telescopic scope and leather shoulder sling made it seem both more real and more magical than our own guns. It was a vision of ourselves as heroic hunters that kept us digging that weekend, despite the blisters forming under our gloves and the sweat trickling down our ribs as we labored to heave the dirt out of the deepening hole. Jonathan and Peter stood around and watched as Bill and I dug, but they weren't part of the story. Only ten and eight, they were still kids. Their job was to envy us, who, even with this mundane-seeming task of digging with pick and shovel, had actually already begun an initiation that would set us apart from them, would place a huge, longed-for gulf between our childhoods and our future. This would be our first deer-hunting season; this, we sensed, would be a crucial passage into manhood for us both.

I'd been hunting for what seemed a long time before that day. I was given my first gun, a .410 gauge shotgun, by my father when I was ten. My .22 rifle had a pump action and could hold eight rounds, and was fashioned from a new alloy that made it so light it almost seemed toylike.

On a typical spring day of that year, when the four of us got off the school bus, we'd go our own ways. Bill would close himself in his room and listen to records or pop music on his radio. Jon and Peter would wander off to play together or maybe watch TV. Mom was usually busy with Nancy, who was only four. I'd change out of my school clothes and, while still in my stockinged feet, slip into the library where all three rifles were kept on a pale pine gun rack. (My father's loaded pistol was in his office desk drawer in the next room.) The library was a dark room, three walls floor to ceiling with bookshelves; the fourth had a green floral couch with the gun rack mounted above it. As I balanced unsteadily on the couch cushions and reached up for my rifle, the pine supports were like open white hands emerging from the wall to offer it to me. The ammunition boxes were in a small, unlocked drawer at the base of the rack. I'd slip a box of bullets into my windbreaker pocket, put on my sneakers, and be out the door in minutes, headed for the woods that bordered our yard on two sides.

I'd roam the woods for hours, until dusk or cold forced me home. These excursions were motivated half by a passion for wandering in the woods, half by a desperate loneliness that weighed me down. When I was in the woods, I felt free and released from a vague misery I didn't understand. My dream of being in the woods involved absolute silence, and every footfall that crackled leaves or snapped twigs bothered me. I wasn't happy until I found a fallen log where I could sit for a long time without moving or making a sound. I wanted to be so still I would become invisible, so that the woods would return to the state they'd been in before I arrived and the animals would move about as if I weren't even there. I wanted to sit so still and breathe so softly that I became only a pair of eyes gazing out into the woods, alert to the fall of a leaf or the distant call of a jay. That much of my dream was benign—the fantasy of my body becoming transparent or vanishing entirely, to be replaced by nothing but focused wonder and the will to observe. It was a desire and pleasure I'd felt for years growing up in the country, miles from the nearest village. But now I carried a gun and that weapon aroused a counter-spirit from somewhere inside me—something as dark and hard as the rifle itself. Now, when I sat on a log, the rifle across my lap had the feel and weight of a king's scepter, and I felt the terrible thrill of power. Now when I was successful at blending into the woods and a gray squirrel, scrabbling about in fallen hickory leaves for nuts, blundered close enough, I'd shoot it.

Why? For the thrill of power. For that terrible and awesome moment when I altered the world with the littlest movement of my finger. I, a shy, tongue-tied kid, might have been the Czar of all Russia and the squirrel some fur-clad peasant trembling in my terrifying presence; I might have been Zeus himself unloosing thunderbolts on some unsuspecting mortal. But why had I killed the squirrel? I had no use for a dead squirrel. I wasn't going to skin it, or eat it. It wasn't a trophy I was going to bring home. There wasn't even anyone I could brag to about my prowess as a hunter. Every time I shot one, I felt the same thing—even as I stood there holding my prize in my hand, I felt my pride draining away faster than the heat of its small body and, flooding in to take the place of my brief vanity, a guilty remorse and self-accusation.

3

The Accident

WHAT WERE JONATHAN AND PETER DOING UP AT THIS HOUR? It was only six in the morning, still dark out. They should be asleep; they didn't have to get ready for school for another hour yet. Bill and I wouldn't be going to school today—the first pleasure of a day that promised many more. Already, the two of us were bundled up in sweaters, coats, and hats, with flashlights stuffed in our pockets. Padded like that, we looked fat as snowmen in the small front hall. But why were Jon and Peter standing there in their pajamas, getting in the way? As Dad came down the stairs with his own rifle, Peter yelled out:

"Why can't we go? It's not fair."

"What do you mean it's not fair?" Bill snapped.

"Go away."

I did my best to bat one of them away as if he were a small, yapping dog, but the room was too crowded for anyone to move easily. Mom was there, too, retying Bill's bootlaces.

"Why can't we go?" they both howled at once.

"Because this is for grown-ups, and you're just kids," I said with utter contempt. And as if to prove my point, they both began crying.

By now, Bill and I were both shouting that they were just crybabies and should shut up and get out of our way. Dad had stopped on a lower step of the stairs and surveyed the chaotic room as if it was a puddle he'd meant to cross, but suddenly had the thought that it was deeper than he'd anticipated and maybe wading in wasn't such a good idea. Bill's and my screams weren't having the desired effect of silencing Peter and Jon, and it looked as if they might go on indefinitely, when Mom looked up at Dad and said: "Jim, maybe they could go just this one time."

At that suggestion, Bill and I were even more furious. As if there would be a "next time"—wasn't this our only chance to have a first day of deer-hunting season? Wasn't it something so special that Dad, who never took a day off from morning house calls to be with us, had done so today? Why should we share it with them? They didn't belong and we said so.

But we could sense that shift taking place that so often resulted when Mom entered into our childish bickering with her reasonable justice that tended toward compassion for the weaker party. Bill and I had no choice but to start whining ourselves, as if we were the more righteous and injured. But Dad cut it all short from the stairs: "OK, they can go. But everyone pipe down. And the two of you—get dressed pronto."

They whooped their way up the stairs, while Bill and I muttered and shared one of our rare moments of communion and agreement: the kids, we were certain, were bound to ruin the trip. With them along, we might as well invite Mom, too, and even Nancy, who was only four. Why not bring the dog and the cats, too? Why not have a picnic?

It had been a clear night and was still dark as the five of us started our march along the dirt road and then out over the frosted field grass that made a crunching sound underfoot. To keep my ears from the bitter cold, I'd pulled my hood down so that I had no more than a small, fur-bordered porthole through which to view the world. I kept my eyes on Dad's boots silhouetted in his wavering flashlight beam and tried my best to ignore the frigid air that fit like a thin mask of ice over the exposed parts of my face.

A faint, gray light was just seeping up from the eastern horizon as we arrived at our trench. Our whole group paused there as Bill, Dad, and I removed our gloves and each loaded a single shell into his rifle. My hands trembled with cold and excitement as I slid the hollow-point bullet into the chamber of my .22 and clicked on the safety catch that would prevent any accidental firing until I was ready to shoot. We set the rifles on the ground beside us and began the awkward clambering down into our hillside excavation that had been dug by two somewhat lazy workers to hold three and was now being asked to accommodate five. It did so somehow and packed us in so tight that what we lost in mobility we gained in body heat.

Now, all was silence broken only by whispers and the occasional distant caw of crows. As the gray light grew, I watched the frost flowers scattered across the dirt mound a few inches from my face melt like the stars going out overhead. I watched my breath rise up in wisps like the mist off the dew-drenched reeds. I waited as patiently as I could. And then we saw it: a deer slowly working its way along the trail through the power-line swamp and out into the field below us, where it paused to browse the short grass. An antlered buck! Dad whispered that Bill would shoot first. This order, if a whispered statement could be called an order, stunned me. What could he possibly mean? Was this another one of those "you'll have your chance when you're older" routines? Did he mean that if Bill missed, I could shoot? Or did he imagine that our luck would be so extraordinary that if Bill killed this deer, a second one would appear this same morning? Surely he couldn't imagine that I would wait for another day. There was no time to explain to Dad how wrong-headed he was being. No time to tell him I *had* to take part, that it would be impossible for me not to shoot at this deer, too. As Bill put his rifle to his shoulder and took aim at the deer, I, too, lifted my .22 with the one bullet in the chamber and sighted along the barrel. And when Bill fired, I fired too, at the exact same instant, so that our two rifles made a single harsh sound that echoed off the woods as the deer collapsed in the green field.

Whooping and yelling, the five of us scrambled down the brush-grown slope and raced to where the deer lay dead in the low grass of the field. We stood around it in a loose circle of awe. By now, my father had calmed down.

"Check your chambers," he said.

At this command, each of us was supposed to point his rifle straight down at the ground and pull the trigger to make sure the gun was empty. If, by some mischance, the bullet had misfired, then the gun would discharge harmlessly into the dirt at our feet. But I was still delirious with glee at what I had accomplished, since it was obvious to me that I, too, not just Bill, had brought down our quarry. I *knew* my pulling the trigger now would only produce the dull mechanical click of a firing pin in an empty chamber.

I was wrong. In my excitement after the deer fell, I must have clicked the safety off again and now, instead of pointing my rifle barrel at the ground, I casually directed it back over my right shoulder toward the woods and never even looked as I pulled the trigger. And Peter was there, a little behind me, not more than two feet from where I stood. In that instant in which the sound of my gun firing made me startle and look around, Peter was already lying motionless on the ground at my feet. I never saw his face—only his small figure lying there, the hood up over his head, a dark stain of blood already seeping across the fabric toward the fringe of fur riffling in the breeze. I never saw his face again.

I screamed. We were all screaming. I don't know what the others were screaming, but I was screaming "I didn't mean to, I didn't mean to!" My father was yelling that we must run for help. I started off across the field toward the house as fast as I could. I ran straight across the swampy stream that split the field and scrambled up the bank and through the barbed-wire fence. I felt Bill and Jon running behind me. I was trying to get to the house first, as if somehow that could help, but what I had done and seen was racing behind me and I couldn't outrun it. That's what I wanted to do: run so fast that I could somehow outrun the horror itself and reach some place where it had never happened, where the world was still innocent of this deed and word of it might never arrive. But I knew that wasn't possible and that even now I was desperately running toward more horror, toward the moment when I would reach the house and when, no matter how exhausted and out of breath I was, I would still have to tell my mother that I had shot Peter.

I hid in my room, hysterical with horror and terror. I lay on my bed, curled up in a ball, howling and crying. I never saw Dad cross the lawn carrying Peter in his arms. An hour later, dizzy with sobbing, I did get up and go to my window at the sound of the siren and the sight of the pale green ambulance backing up to our front door. I did glimpse the stretcher being slid inside, but Peter's body was hidden by blankets and the white-coated backs of the ambulance people.

I couldn't leave my room. I kept returning to the bed and curling up, clutching my pillow and sobbing into it or crying and biting it. I kept my eyes closed as much as I could, as if by doing that I could hide from my family and the horrible new reality I had brought into the world. It was as if I thought that by keeping my eyes shut and staying curled up on my bed, I could cancel out the world and the people around me. But with my eyes closed I kept seeing Peter's body on the ground and I found myself pleading with my parents in my imagination, begging them to forgive me for what I had done. It was an indescribably painful ordeal, but at least it was taking place inside the privacy of my own mind. I thought I would die if I had to actually look at my parents or anyone in my family. And so I lay in a ball of agony on my bed and hoped no one would enter my room.

But eventually, several hours after the ambulance left, someone did. It was my mother.

"Greg," she began.

"I'm sorry. I'm sorry. Please, go away." I begged.

"Greg, it was an accident. It was a terrible accident. It wasn't your fault."

I started sobbing all over again. What she said made no sense. Of course it was my fault. Did she think I was stupid—that I didn't know what I had done, didn't know that I had done it? You could say that spilling soda was an accident, but you couldn't say that killing your brother was an accident. That was something far more horrible than an accident. Nothing in the word "accident" offered me any hope. But what she said next was even worse:

"Something very much like this happened to your father when he was your age."

"What do you mean?"

"He killed a friend of his in a hunting accident."

She said it that simply, though it couldn't have been easy for her to say, any more than it could have been easy for her to visit my room. She had been standing all this time by my desk, about five feet from my bed. Her deep-set eyes were red from her own sobbing, and she stood with her arms crossed on her chest as if she were trying to hold herself together, to keep from bursting apart with grief. She was speaking to me about this strange and awful coincidence, but her voice was numb and distant, as if she were repeating it to herself simply to hear it spoken aloud, to see if it sounded believable. It didn't. Not to me. That is, it sounded unbelievable and terrible, but this was exactly the world I had now entered with my stupid mistake: the world of the terrible and unbelievable. I had killed my own brother. Why not learn this also—that my father had once killed someone, too? I heard what she said. I wanted to ask what she meant, but I couldn't speak. I just lay there moaning. She stood for a while by my bed and then she left the room, closing the door behind her.

I had wanted her to hold me, but I couldn't say that. I had wanted her to forgive me, but I couldn't ask. I felt as if I had lost her love forever.

Hours later, early in the afternoon, there was a knock on the door of my room. It was Bethany, my father's receptionist, with a tray of soup. I was so hungry that my hunger overcame my shame, and I sat on the edge of the bed with the tray on my lap, slurping it down but unable to look up or say anything, She must have brought the soup from her home, because it had a taste I didn't recognize. While I ate, she stood far back by the door and waited.

"This is an awful thing, Greg, but you should know that right now Peter is in heaven with Jesus."

I stopped eating. I just sat there waiting, unable to believe I had heard her say that. I covered my face with both hands, but I was too exhausted or dehydrated to cry anymore. Still, when I closed my eyes I saw Peter and he was not sitting on Jesus' lap and gazing up into Christ's mild countenance as the lamb did in the stained glass window in our church. Instead, Peter was lying face down on the cold ground in the field. I knew she was only trying to comfort me and to tell me what she believed, but it had the opposite effect. I thought she was crazy. I wanted to say: "What's wrong with you? Didn't you see his body? Don't you know what happened? Don't you know he's dead?" I wanted to scream at her: "This isn't Sunday school! My brother was just killed by a bullet and I fired it. What kind of nonsense are you saying?"

"It may not make sense now," she continued, "but it's all part of God's plan."

I hadn't thought much about God, hadn't yet had much reason to, but when Bethany dredged up out of her rural heart the strongest consolations she could find to set against my obvious suffering and terror, she inadvertently ended forever any hope I had of conventional religious belief. What she said seemed like a simple-minded mockery of what I had seen and done. Maybe if she hadn't spoken so soon after Peter's death, I could have found the intended comfort in what she said. Maybe if my mother had held me when she visited, had given me some reassurance that I was not a monster, I would have been more receptive to Bethany's story of supernatural resurrection and a benevolent though mysterious plan that governed the universe. Instead, I felt rage and despair. Either this was a meaningless and horrible universe and this woman's ideas were a lollipop she sucked in the dark, or else there was a divine plan, but it was not benevolent. What had my mother meant about my father having killed someone too? How could my father and I have done the same horrible thing at the same age? Certainly that coincidence represented some mysterious, even supernatural pattern, but who could imagine it being a happy pattern, a pattern that showed there was a God and he cared about us humans?

I had one last unwelcome visitor that day. A state trooper arrived to complete the investigation into Peter's death. My father appeared at my door:

"You should know that he died in the ambulance and that he never recovered consciousness. That means he didn't suffer."

He asked me to come down to his office. It was part of a three-room complex at the back of the house that included a waiting room and a small examining room. The office was an interior room. Its only light came from a brass table lamp with a green glass shade that cast a small pool at its base. As we entered the shadowy room, my father moved to a place in a corner, where he stood without saying anything. The trooper was seated awkwardly at my father's desk, which was far too small for him. Even his hat was outsized and out of place, flopped down on the desktop like a giant, brooding spider. The trooper was a young man with a blond crewcut and an open, beefy face. He was awkward and embarrassed and, except for a brief glance when I first entered and sat down, he never looked at me again. Instead, he sat with his forehead propped on one hand and his face bowed over the forms. He looked like a school kid unsure of his handwriting and so concentrating entirely on the act of moving his pen across the paper.

"What happened, son?"

"I don't know."

When I said this, it seemed as close to the truth as I could come, but I wasn't going to be allowed to stop there.

"Start at the beginning. How did it happen?"

"We were hunting."

"Who is we?"

I sat hunched in the chair by the desk. My eyes kept blurring. The neat row of bullets wedged into their individual loops on his gunbelt became a centipede crawling across his belly. The mahogany swivel chair he sat in had belonged to my father's father, a man who died when I was a baby. There was a brass plaque mounted on its back that said it was the chair he'd sat in when he served as superintendent of prisons for New York State from 1915 to 1919. Now it seemed to foretell my own fate as I stared at the trooper's handcuffs dangling over the edge of the seat.

"Tell me what happened, son."

He was here to investigate and file a report on Peter's death—to me, Peter's murder. He was here to investigate a crime that I had committed. All afternoon I had struggled to believe that what had happened had not happened, could not happen, was too horrible to have happened. Every time I had closed my eyes I had seen Peter's body on the ground, had felt the rifle in my hands. That moment had stopped forever, frozen in my brain. But that suspended moment seemed a private horror. Now this trooper, who represented society and the world of other people, was asking me to publicly acknowledge with my own words that it *had* happened. He was asking me to confess, to admit to the whole world that I had done the inconceivable: I had killed my own brother.

For the first time I saw that I was trapped forever. Once I had spoken the words of the narrative that linked me to my brother's death, once they had been written down in an official report, my guilt and shame would be absolute and ineradicable. I had destroyed my family with my careless act, and now I would stand before the world and my monstrosity would be revealed by my own words. I wanted to be silent, to never speak again, just as I wanted to hide in my room forever. But this trooper, with his embarrassed patience, was forcing me to say the words that would make Peter's death real to everyone.

"Try again, son. I know it's not easy. What do you remember?"

"We were hunting. We shot a deer . . . "

Each word I spoke was innocent. Each sentence seemed harmless in itself. Yet each one moved me closer to my brother's corpse and there was no escape. If I could lie! If I could shout: "It wasn't loaded! My gun was empty!" or "I didn't pull the trigger. It must have been someone else." Would that have saved me? Or if I said nothing at all? If I simply sat there in silence and refused to speak, would someone else have been blamed?

No, I was going to be destroyed for my crime. Revenge was swift and self-inflicted. I would convict myself with my own words. There would be no trial, no need for a trial: here was judge and jury, here was my father who stood for our family, and the trooper who stood for the world outside my family—our neighbors, the town, the county, all those who had a right to know a monster lived among them.

And so I spoke the words of my story, confused as it was. I was sick to my stomach with the horror of what I had done, and sick too with the shame of confessing it aloud, and with fear of the punishment that must follow.

4

Meanings

IT'S NOT POSSIBLE TO LIVE IN A WORLD WITHOUT MEANING.
Or at least I don't think I could. I know that as a twelve-year-old child
I needed meanings to understand my life. But all the meanings, all the
childish understandings of life that had sustained me up until that day
were suddenly and completely eradicated by Peter's death. My whole
understanding of the world, my whole sense that the world was under-
standable, vanished in the immediate aftermath of this catastrophe. I
know my father carried Peter's body out of the field, that it was placed
in an ambulance and taken to the hospital and from there to the funeral home. But to me, his body was still in the field. Whenever I closed
my eyes that day, I saw his body lying there. In this vision seared into
my brain, my rifle no longer lay beside him and I was standing further
back, in a shadowy place about six feet away from where he was curled
up on his side. But I was powerless to stop staring at his small form, to
break my gaze from the magnetic hold of it where he lay as if asleep on
the preternaturally green grass of that field. And I knew without looking up that the surrounding woods had vanished, that the hill and our
distant house no longer existed. I knew that everything else in the world
had been obliterated by the stillness of his body.

Could anything have saved me from that sense of absolute desolation on the day of Peter's death and in the days and years that followed it? I think if someone had held me at some point during that day, it would have helped; it would have given me some animal comfort. I think if a person had been able to break through my shell of terror and shame and spoken to me out of their own human brokenness and confusion, it would have helped. I felt as if I was in free fall through the Void. I needed arms to catch me. I needed some voice to tell me I was not alone. I needed my parents to be there with me to save me from the accusing voices in my head that were shouting, "Murderer, murderer!"

But the voices and human presences I yearned for so desperately could not be there when I needed them. My father and mother must each have retreated into their own sense of horror, despair, and guilt. My father must have been remembering how only a month before, his wife's parents had visited us on their way south for the winter, and my grandfather, a combat veteran of World War I who had himself seen horror and breathed poison gas in the shattered forests of the Argonne, had taken him aside and said: "Jim, you can't have all these guns loose around the house with all these kids. Someone is going to get hurt." And my mother must have remembered again and again saying to my father that morning: "Jim, maybe they could go just this one time." Both of them must immediately have thought of the strange parallel event from my father's childhood. And there were other family tragedies that I didn't and couldn't know about then. It's no wonder my parents weren't able to be near me that day. I know my mother tried, but perhaps she was too stunned herself; what she did manage to say only confused me more and deepened my despair.

Yes, I begged people to leave me alone that day, but when they did it denied me that most basic sustaining force: the warmth of being wrapped in human arms, of someone speaking to me—not coherent words perhaps, but just the soothing repetitions of sound, the "there, there" with which a child is calmed who has woken from a nightmare. But for me, from that moment, the world was nightmare and there was no waking from it.

Peter's death wiped out all the easy meanings I had lived by until that day, as if a giant hand swept the counters and dice of a child's game off the board. But this hand, with its single swipe, wiped the board itself clean of its orderly squares, and all that was on them the chutes and ladders, the neat lettering on certain squares inviting you to roll again, the reassuring declarations of "start" and "finish." All this was wiped out by the single movement of the giant hand and the board itself was now a terrifying blank square. What now? How was I to orient myself on a board as bare and empty as an Arctic ice floe? What meaning was strong enough to set against this sinister glare, blank and blind as an eye glazed over with cataract?

God, Bethany's God, was not believable to me—this God who was already setting a place for Peter at his heavenly feast table before my brother's body was even buried in this world. Such an instant and naive solution to suffering seemed repellent and unreal. Even if I could have imagined it before Peter's death, now that I had been a part of this horror, I couldn't believe in anything as simple as this God who was portrayed as a smiling dinner host. Still, Bethany had also spoken of another aspect of her God—that he knew and understood everything and he had a plan into which even Peter's death fit. This plan, Bethany implied, was benevolent and purposeful in a way we mortals couldn't, because of our limits, comprehend, something grand and sacred that only a god could grasp.

If there was no plan, if the game board really had become irrevocably blank, then I had nothing to hold on to but that single, other word people had used to explain what happened: "accident." If there was no plan, then maybe the god who ruled this world was named Accident, a god who joyed in randomness, who ripped apart lives for no reason, who swallowed stars and toyed with the Void.

But this was an insupportable idea. How could I live in a world where everything was random, where Accident ruled and where one day I might wake to sunshine and blue sky and another, find my own brother dead at my feet? Accident. Unbearable word, unbearable world.

And so, I came back to Bethany's God. But maybe her God was different than she, in her naive goodness, believed. Maybe he wasn't merely a designer of obscurely comprehended but benevolent plans—no, but a God even more inscrutable, with a penchant for making sinister, incomprehensible patterns. Patterns like this: I killed Peter with a gun, just as my father, years before, when he was my age, had also killed an unknown someone with a gun.

If not for a god, a strange and dangerous god, how could anyone explain a repetition as bizarre as this? My father and then myself—each performing the same, almost unimaginable deed. Here was a chilling and compelling pattern right before my eyes. I might not believe God could lift Peter out of the morgue to dine at his celestial banquet, but how could I doubt that this violent coincidence was full of meaning? And wasn't that what I wanted and desperately needed that day of Peter's death: a world where meaning existed?

I decided that there must be a God who had willed this pattern, and that for some reason he had turned his other face toward me: his merciless aspect, riven with mysterious shadows. I had a choice: I could try to live without meaning, or I could bow before this God. I bowed.

5

Child Mind

I DON'T KNOW HOW ADULT MINDS ARRIVE AT MEANINGS. I don't know what they need, or how they figure things out. But here are two stories about children and how they think. When my wife, as a child, first heard the opening phrase of the prayer "Our Father who art in Heaven," she imagined a bearded man wearing a smock and a beret, holding a paintbrush in one hand, a palette in the other, and standing before an easel. And why not? Here was a Creator God. Here is the figure who might well have painted the bright primary arc of the rainbow as a symbol of his good intentions toward his people. I'm not surprised my wife became a painter.

The other story about how children think isn't so charming and benign. I heard it from my younger brother, Jonathan, only recently, when he learned I was writing this book. It was a story he had never told anyone except his wife in all the time since the accident. The week of Peter's death, Jonathan was scheduled to have a math test that he knew he couldn't possibly pass. That Sunday evening, before he climbed into bed, he prayed to God: "God, if you just get me out of this math test, I will never ask you for anything else again. Just help me this once, please." We didn't go to school that week after the accident, and when we finally did, Jon's math test was long forgotten.

As Jon sat in his room, as he watched neighbors enter to dismantle Peter's brass bed and carry it out to be stored in the barn, as the slow days went by and he tried to comprehend what had taken place, an awful realization dawned on him: God *had* answered his prayer. God had heard his selfish request and had granted it by killing Peter.

6

Numb

I WAS NUMB AT THE FUNERAL. I REMEMBER ALMOST NOTHING except a white curtain that was drawn to keep us, the family, separate from the rest of the mourners. We sat in a little alcove. I remember the chairs—the same folding metal ones I'd set up or folded countless times in the school gym or at Cub Scouts or in church basements. I don't remember people, except as a kind of whispering around me. And where was I? I was deep in a desert wilderness as desolate as that inhabited by those early, God-tormented, Christian saints who lived their whole lives alone on top of stone columns. Only I wasn't on top of the column, I was embedded inside it, as if it were a shaft of pure shame transparent as Lucite, and I was immobilized inside it, like an insect or some unusual beetle. I heard people whispering around me like the desert breeze around the pillar, but I couldn't move or look up, and so as far as I could tell no one was there.

The gravesite was a two-hour drive from our town—across the Hudson and north into the Heldeberg Hills southwest of Albany, where we had lived when I was first born. As we drove home, in the dark, I felt my faith in the devouring God grow stronger. I saw that Death, his angel, was everywhere, that it had entered our lives and I had opened the door to welcome it. I saw that it could enter in the spectacular, terrible form of Peter's violent death, but that it could also insinuate itself in minor ways, in numberless tiny shapes you might not even notice until they had worked their way toward a beating heart in order to still it. Sitting in the dark in the backseat during that long drive, I saw that death was with us. It was the small white snail of wadded Kleenex my mother kept pressing against her face; it was nibbling holes in her cheek as if it was a leaf. I saw that death was the moonlight's patch of blue mold growing on my father's shoulder as he drove, oblivious, through the deep night.

When I tried to sleep that night and for years after, I could only do so if I began in one position: flat on my back with my arms crossed on my chest and my legs hooked over each other at the ankles. Lying like that in the dark room, in the pose of a mummy in an Egyptian sarcophagus, I calmed myself toward sleep. I imagined I was both the body inside, immobilized by its wrapping of thin linen strips, and the wooden case itself, painted with the expressionless face and figure of its dead occupant. I was afraid of my thoughts and afraid of the dark. I needed a double magic of rigidity to brace me against the violent storms of my dreams.

7

The Field

IN MY DREAM, I HEARD GOD'S VOICE DEMANDING, "WHAT *have you done with your brother?" His question was like a fiery finger poking a hole through my chest, through my life. I saw the Bible they'd given me years ago in my first Sunday school, with its black leatherette cover stamped at the top in large gold letters "Holy Bible" and at the bottom "Gregory Orr" in a tiny font. A slow-motion bullet approached the book from behind and struck the back cover dead center, entering it in a ragged hole but not emerging on the other side. Now the book was a black wall I was facing and the bullet hole had become the entrance to a cave. I walked through the tunnel, listening to whispers from the tissue-thin pages that had been torn to incoherence. I could feel that the book's later meanings had been destroyed by the bullet, especially those that offered hope and redemption. It had penetrated all the way to the earliest pages and now I had to follow its path. I walked for hours through darkness. The whispering disappeared. I saw nothing and heard only the sound of my own breathing. Then far ahead there was a dim red glow that grew brighter as I approached and suddenly, I was standing in a hollow space stained with ancient blood. I heard again our horrified screams as my gun fired, and I saw Cain standing above his brother, Abel, bleeding to death in a field.*

8

Cain Continuing

FRIGHTENING AS MY DREAM OF CAIN WAS, IT OFFERED ME hope by offering me the shelter of a story. And stories are where human meanings begin. If I were Cain, I knew who I was and where I was situated in the universe. I was the one who had slain his brother. I was the one God was angry at. But he would not kill me. The story didn't go in that direction. Instead, he would drive me alone into the wilderness. And wasn't that how I felt? Isolated, alone. Shunned by people. Townspeople and my fellow students were, like my parents, afraid to speak to me. They probably felt sorry for me, but I didn't know that. I thought they were afraid of me, because they saw my brother's blood on my hands, sensed the uncanniness of Cain—that he was picked out by God to commit a terrible crime. I felt abandoned by my parents, but no one harmed me. Even the trooper had not arrested me. It was as if I wore the mark of Cain. It was a worse punishment for Cain to live than it would have been for him to die: "a fugitive and a vagabond shalt thou be in the earth."

"And Cain said unto the Lord, 'My punishment is greater than I can bear.'" But God would not let Cain die and he would not let anyone punish me. He knew that my own self-hatred was a far more terrible punishment.

Like Cain, I would be allowed to live and to live in a world of meaning, though it was a meaning that filled me with despair. The story of Cain satisfied my childish needs by placing me at the center of a story. I was a child and believed that the world, if it made sense at all, made sense with me as the central character.

I didn't know that other people were making up other stories to explain Peter's death. In my child's egoism, I couldn't realize my parents had lives and fates of their own, distinct from mine. It never occurred to me that they might believe that their own actions had brought them to this place.

Part Two

9

Alcove

DASHING, SPONTANEOUS, IRREPRESSIBLE, MY FATHER, JAMES Wendell Orr, must have swept my mother off her feet when they first met. He was darkly handsome, with thick black hair, dense eyebrows, and an open, grinning face. Everything about his manner said that life was fun in a wild kind of way and should be enjoyed. Coming from her pinch-faced, teetotaling New England background, my mother couldn't possibly have ever seen anyone like him before. Grammie Howe, my mother's mother, hated him from the start, which may have made him only that much more irresistible to my mother. Within months of their meeting, my parents were married.

My father's father had begun as a homeless newsboy on the streets of Detroit and risen to become city editor of the *New York Tribune,* and later, secretary to the governor of New York. My own father had grown up as the spoiled youngest child of his rich Yonkers family.

Somewhere in the story of my father's privileged childhood something is missing: is it a simple bump in the road, or a secret point on which his whole life pivoted? Somewhere in his early adolescence is his own story of responsibility for the sudden death of a loved one. It is not a story he has ever told to anyone I know. Not a single word about it has ever passed between him and myself in all these years. My mother spoke her single, cryptic sentence about it to me the day of Peter's death, and then she, too, would never mention it again. I could tell from the way she spoke that it was a dark and shameful secret. And yet, now I do know something about it; I even know the victim's name. Six years ago, I called my father's older sister, a woman I knew as Aunt Doe. She and my father hadn't talked in forty years, though I didn't know why.

"Aunt Doe," I said, "this is your nephew Greg. If you don't mind, I need to ask you an odd question."

"Well, go ahead."

"When Peter died, my mother told me something like that had happened to my father, too, but she never said what. Do you know anything about that?"

"You mean, your parents never told you about Charley Hayes?" she asked incredulously. No, I assured her; I had never even heard his name before. And she told me all she knew:

"Charley and your father were inseparable. They were best friends. They must have been ten at the time. It was at our country house; we'd just come up the day before from Yonkers. The two of them snuck a rifle out of the house, one that the chauffeur kept in the trunk of the Packard. And some paper plates from the kitchen— they were going to go skeet shooting in a back field, you know, throw the plates into the air and pretend they were clay pigeons. Then it happened, somehow your father shot Charley. We don't really know the details of it. Your father ran back to the house and then the chauffeur went out to the field and carried Charley's body back. Your grandmother packed us up that same day and took us back to the city. I don't know whether that was right or not, but something like that is so terrible. It was awful. I can't believe they never told you about it when Peter died. It was the first thing we all thought about, the awful coincidence of it."

And that was all she could tell me, though I sensed in her voice questions about how her family had responded to Charley's death, whether Dad's mother was right to whisk them so quickly back to the city. Behind that act, I could sense a familial response I knew from my own childhood: the sudden flight from the scene that is the first, concrete step toward denial of the horror.

And so, my father's adolescence continued. Even in the middle of the Depression, he was dropped off by the chauffeured Packard at a fancy New York private school. By the time he went on to Hamilton College, his spirited and irresponsible tendencies had acquired a wilder, more dramatic cast. He flunked out before the end of his first year, then started over at Columbia College. But shortly after, when World War II began, he joined the Navy Air Force and was sent to Ithaca for flight training.

My mother's maiden name was Barbara Howe. Her solid, straight-laced family traced itself back, with somber vanity, to an English ship that arrived off the coast of Massachusetts in 1630. My mother's father worked as an executive for Boston Sand and Gravel, devoting his bland working life to selling off by the truckload soil mingled with his ancestors' bones. Somehow it was apt—except for his big adventure as a young man in the First World War, he himself was a colorless, basic man who might have been made of the substances he sold. After high school, my mother became a scholarship student in architecture at MIT. I've tried to imagine her back then—what a serious, even brilliant student she must have been to have gained entrance into that bastion of male science and technology back in those pre-feminist days. In her high school graduation portrait, she's wearing a string of pearls and a simple, short-sleeved sweater. She has a wide, plain face, high cheekbones, and clear, intelligent eyes that make her quite beautiful in an unassuming way. In the photo, she's wearing her hair in braids wrapped around the top of her head like a rustic halo. After her first year at MIT, America entered the Second World War and she was lured to

Cornell by the Curtiss-Wright Aircraft Company, which was training women to work in aircraft design. It was there she met my father and by the time he was transferred to navigation training in Indiana, they were married.

In Indiana, he ran into disciplinary trouble and washed out. He started over again, testing so well that he was put in a "Ninety-Day Wonder" school at Northwestern University that put extraordinary enlisted men through intensive officer training and graduated them as ensigns. Again, he misbehaved and was demoted, though he somehow managed to graduate. From there, he was sent to underwater demolition training in Florida. One night, he smuggled my mother onto the base disguised in a sailor's uniform and took her out with his crew and several cases of beer for a midnight cruise in the small landing craft he commanded. Drunk, they ran across a coral head and sank ten yards off a beach. He somehow escaped the full consequences of that escapade, only to find himself at war's end on Guam, without ever having fired or been fired upon.

When Dad returned to the States, he went back to Columbia, where he was still only a sophomore. But he was admitted—rather inexplicably he thought—into medical school while he was still a junior pre-med. As far as he knows, he never completed his undergraduate degree but simply moved on in the confusion of all the servicemen returning to school on the GI Bill.

In the winter of 1947, when I was born, he and Mom were living in a farmhouse without indoor plumbing or hot water and heated only with a woodstove. The farmhouse was near the hamlet of Alcove in the rugged Heldeberg Hills thirty miles southwest of Albany, where my Dad was enrolled in Albany Medical College. The one-story farmhouse was ramshackle, and the unpainted barn, where Mom kept her herd of goats, two dozen rabbits, and a milk cow, was even more dilapidated. What had been an apple orchard behind the house was long abandoned, and my first memory is of climbing onto a rusting truck that rested under one of these unpruned trees, bristling and scabbed with neglect. Still, the landscape had a bleak kind of beauty, according to my father, and the hay field in front of the house gave a view down to the pine-flanked Alcove reservoir where the occasional bald eagle was still seen.

I was the third baby boy born in as many years. That first winter of my life the house still had no furnace and no hot water—my mother washed our diapers in cold water hand-pumped into the kitchen sink. How odd it must have been for these two children of urban privilege to have chosen such a place to begin their lives together. Why didn't they rent an apartment in Albany? Or a house in its suburbs? The only explanation my father has ever offered for their living in such primitive circumstances was that he'd had enough of close quarters with other sailors in the war and when he came back he wanted to live as far from people and crowds as possible. What my mother thought of it, I'll never know.

Although alcohol fueled almost all the escapades that unraveled so disastrously and in such rapid succession during my father's young adulthood, it had utterly vanished by the time I was born. The rash and passionate relationship with booze which had come close to wrecking his young life a dozen times had been replaced by something else.

Early on in his medical school days, my father discovered amphetamine. What a miracle this powdered electricity compressed into little tablets must have been to him, as it was to countless other overworked medical students and interns—what a descent of grace, what balm in Gilead, what an oasis of green energy in the gray wastes of his daily exhaustion and stress! The endless complex studying and exams, the red-eyed, round-the-clock ward duties, the long drives home, and the labor on the farm as well—all these responsibilities that rose up and promised to overwhelm him now receded before this potent chemical that unlocked the mysteries of the human brain so that a man was turned into a demigod and a mortal gained knowledge and concentrated powers a god would envy. Holy tablets more precious than gold—my father hugged them closer than Moses gripped those flat stones God himself inscribed.

Those pills so saturated my father's life that they seemed to have the power to appear anywhere, like mushrooms on a green lawn. Years later, my father drove me to my first day at college. We'd just pulled into the freshman dorm parking lot and I'd begun to unload suitcases from the back seat when he lifted from the open trunk a large, opaque plastic jug. "Here," he said, "this might come in handy," and he transferred it to me. It weighed six pounds and had to be carried in the crook of my arm like a small baby. It could have been an industrial-sized jar of ketchup or some other condiment, but it wasn't—it was a bottle of one thousand amphetamine tablets, an extravagant parting gift from a man ordinarily noted for stinginess.

In the short time we spent unloading my stuff in the dorm, he gave me my first full sermon on the gospel of speed, though there had been hints before—casual, grim quips like: "Unhappy? We can give you a whole new chemical personality." "Unhappy" said with an unctuous, drawn-out tone of concern ending in the diabolical parody of a completely insincere, salesman's grin. And this "we" was all the up-to-date physicians, my father chief among them. Today, our culture is inured to the concept of a chemically-engineered personality, but back then in the early sixties, the phrase shocked and unnerved me. Nor was it reassuring to hear my father so insistently and intently cynical. Some of that cynicism must have emerged from despair: amphetamine in the morning; sleeping pills at night; then amphetamine again as the next morning dawned. My father was a walking, fast-talking endorsement of his grandiose claims, but he was also a partly empty husk sparked by the stuff—a hopped-up, volatile, addicted puppet. Only last year, Jonathan told me that, lying on the living room couch one day when he was ten, he heard my mother shout: "Jim, a mouse!" Dad was napping in his shorts at the time, in one of those frazzled collapses that alternated with his chemical highs. He leapt up, grabbed the .38 he kept in his bedside drawer at the time, ran down the stairs, and began blasting pistol shots at the tiny beast as it scurried among the dining room chairs and Jon screamed for help from the next room only a thin wall away. "Yes," I said, though Jon's anecdote was more overtly violent than any memory I had of that time. Yes, this is the man about whom we'd whisper our encrypted warnings in the dark halls of the house: "Stay away, he's in a bad mood."

Even with amphetamine's chemical assist, my father's struggle to graduate from medical school was immense. When he was still at Columbia, a professor told him that if any medical student lived more than fifteen minutes by subway from Columbia his teachers knew he would flunk out by semester's end. My father often thought about that as he drove his Model T truck the one-hour trip down out of the hills into Albany.

The life my parents lived those years in Alcove wasn't an easy one. It wasn't easy to survive in those circumstances. Not everyone did. Bill, the oldest, was born in 1945; Christopher, a year later, and I the year after that. When Christopher was three years old, he climbed out of his crib in the middle of the night, opened my father's desk drawer, found and swallowed enough pills to poison himself, put the bottle back and closed the drawer, then returned to his bed to sleep. By the time my mother found him comatose the next morning, my father had already left for school. Not until much later that day did they discover what had happened, but by the time they could pump his stomach it was too late. He died the following day.

The one account my father gave of Christopher's death, years later, was so freighted with guilt and shame that I felt guilty myself as I tried to press past the narrative's bare bones. My father's genial countenance distorted into twists and turns, as if half the muscles in his face contracted in a painful effort to focus even as the rest tried to blur and avert his gaze.

"What kind of pills were they?" I asked.

"They were a French antihistamine, little sugar-coated pills Dr. Perkins prescribed for your mother's allergies," he said.

"How did he find them?"

"I don't know. I don't know."

Tortured by my own guilt, I had no stomach for his suffering no matter how much I longed to know more. And yet I saw it clearly—the small boy alone in the room, opening the forbidden drawer. There in the dark, with moonlight from the window leaking in and smearing the edges of things with its cold, mercurial light. He slides it open, that drawer, that narrow rectangle of wood that could have been his coffin if he were smaller. Careless drawer, irresponsible box that gives away so easily its dangerous secrets, that surrenders its poisons so readily. Of course such a drawer is appalling; of course, my father will learn from this and lock up these evil boxes before they can do more harm. And yet he does not—its lesson of jeopardy is one he cannot learn and only ten years later my brother Jonathan will enter my father's bedroom and slip open the distant cousin of Christopher's drawer and lift out the loaded .38 pistol to point around the room, to pretend with.

How can you reason with a drawer, a stupid piece of wood? You can't grab it by the lapels and shake it and scream, "Wake up, don't you see what's going on?" A drawer in a desk doesn't think, it doesn't act, it's not responsible for what happens.

Jon told me the story of my father's mouse hunt in response to my telling him the story of Christopher's death, which he knew only as rumor. I have always been the difficult member of my family—the one whose desperate curiosity about the past irritates and threatens others because it brings back such painful memories. For much of my life, I've felt compelled to probe certain silence-shrouded events and their consequences. It's not a role I chose, but one born out of my own torment and guilt and desire to survive. I wasn't after other people's secrets; all I wanted was information that could be light and clear air. And so, periodically, when the pain got bad, got unbearable, I would ask questions I knew I should not. The last question I dared about Christopher came closest to the agony that dominated my own life:

"How did you and Mom deal with what happened?"

"We didn't. In those days, people didn't talk about things like that. Your mother and I never spoke about him."

So, I was left with a full, empathetic knowledge of how such an awful event must have devastated both of them, but with no model for my own coping. Yet for all their stoic or paralyzed silence, I know Christopher was often in their thoughts. Many years later, I mentioned casually to my father how much I loved the light blue of chicory flowers that, ubiquitous, filled the fields and lined the dusty roads in the Hudson Valley where we lived, and Dad replied: "Christopher's eyes were that color."

10

Renssalaerville

NOT LONG AFTER CHRISTOPHER'S DEATH, WE MOVED OFF the Alcove farm to the nearby village of Renssalaerville. It was still deeper in the Heldebergs, a beautiful village of forty or so clapboard houses strung out along one side of a steep gorge whose stream and waterfalls had powered four separate mills since its founding in the last years of the eighteenth century. When we arrived, only a single, boarded-up relic of that early industrial prosperity still stood; the other three mills were high-walled labyrinths of foundation stones along the banks below the falls. What commerce had long since abandoned, summer wealth still clung to and kept alive— a small "opera house" for Gilbert and Sullivan, a tiny, mahogany-paneled public library, and the Catalpa House, an inn where two dowagers served afternoon tea at white wicker tables on the wide lawn under its namesake trees. And everywhere, like gray threads stitching together the bright quilt of clapboard, lawn, and forest, were long walls of dark, indigenous slate. Grand lines of these piled stones led up each dirt lane; in ramparts it defined sunken hydrangea gardens, or, as high parapets, propped up cottages built out on the very edge of the gorge.

If stone structured the town into sober adultness, it was water's wanderings and flashings that held the younger inhabitants in thrall. About a mile above the village, Lake Miosotis released an outlet stream that meandered through birch and hemlock forest for half a mile until it widened out to slide and glitter over the lip of the falls proper. Seen from the wooden bridge below, the falls rose three hundred feet in thin increments of shale as if it was some celestial staircase for creatures so tiny they'd consume their whole lives climbing toward God. The whole face of the falls was covered with gossamer lace, a foaming, inch-deep scrim of water that glistened and flashed when the sun at last lifted above the edge of the gorge and found it out. Dark hemlocks gazed down over each side until the cliffs became so steep only thick clumps of fern and moss could cling to their dripping walls. Whether you stood in a trance on the bridge or climbed the steep paths, the rich smell of evergreen humus mingled so completely with the ceaseless, quiet roar of the falls it was impossible to separate the two sensations.

At the base of the falls, a smooth-bottomed pool extended a quarter mile down to the village mill dam. Here, the underlying layers of slate were so flat and the stream so shallow that on Saturdays villagers drove their cars right into the water to wash them. In another place, the stream deepened enough to be called the swimming hole.

Further down, where dense thickets of jewelweed clustered along each shore, bullheads had thrashed and fashioned their nesting tunnels into the clay banks. As a kid, groping along that slickness for an opening, I'd thrust my arm in full length, hook my fingers around the cartilaginous barbs that grew behind their whiskers, and yank the primitive, startled creatures out of their holes.

There were other streamside mysteries, too. Caddis fly larvae crawled out on the sun-baked, flat rocks like the dried-up husks of diminutive dragons. Or a minnow cage gleaming on the bottom like a silver-mesh bomb, the tiny trapped fish spinning inside it in frantic, gyroscopic flashes of white belly and orange fin. And once, after spring floods had sluiced the banks, I found a fossil clam perfect as one you might pluck from a fishmonger's bed of chipped ice but made entirely of rock.

It was in Renssalaerville that I started first grade at the age of five. Though it was 1952, the schoolhouse, like the village itself, was lost in time, a pale-planked, churchish structure perched on a hill at the edge of town. Each morning, the bellrope tugged, the brass bell in its squat tower rang its summons out over the ceaseless stream sound.

There were two teachers in two big rooms—a cluster of desks, a blackboard, and a woodstove in each. One teacher taught first, second, and third grades all in the same room on the ground floor; the other taught fourth, fifth, and sixth on the floor above. After sixth, a bus whisked you up the dirt road out of town, over the hills toward Greenville Central's upper grades twenty miles away.

But here, in each room, a score of us labored, oblivious of any larger world except twice a month when the itinerant art teacher appeared and we all crowded into one room. Balding, with a bland, blank face, it was not his figure, but his outfits that shouted the mysteries of art to our small-town eyes: white shirts and bright string ties, one with a silver bull's skull with a red stone glistening in each eye socket. Each lesson began with his announcement of some seasonal theme like spring or Christmas or a patriotic event—especially the births of notable presidents. Armed with crayons and paper, we'd be off to the races. And as if art was a chaotic contest open to all, our teacher, too, put his gifts and imagination to the task at hand. Half an hour later, each student displayed his or her creation, and lo—the winner (how did one win? who judged?) was given the teacher's drawing as a prize! I remember these odd contests well, having once, with my image of little George attacking the cherry tree with his hatchet, won the teacher's own version of Rembrandt Peale's Washington portrait, the one with puffs of white space at the bottom as if he was standing over a steam grate or peering down from clouds.

On alternate weeks, a music teacher appeared. Again, all six grades duly gathered together. These visiting teachers seemed to me to come from some other world far more sophisticated than I could imagine. Perhaps they weren't traveling teachers at all; perhaps they were only local talent hired for the day—but to me they were as amazing and mysterious as circuit-riding preachers who had the power to dazzle us, their widely scattered and benighted flock, with the gospel of art. Although I firmly believed our drawing teacher was a genius, I was even more in awe of the man who taught us music.

At just the right moment, after announcing the song we would all sing, this mystagogue would produce a round, chrome-silver pitch pipe from his vest pocket and blow a single, clear tone. I assume it was the opening note of the song, but since I was incapable of coming within shouting distance of any designated note, it made no difference. Stunned that this gleaming disk enclosed in its mystic circumference an entire musical scale, I'd stare, dumb and vacant as someone hypnotized by a dangled pocket watch as the rest of the class stumbled its way through the melody.

In those days there was nothing about school I didn't love. But most of all I cherished how simple, predictable, and responsive it was. In school, everything made sense and there were no mysteries, no shadows and silences that stirred vague longings in me. Everything was overt and clear, as if lit by a bright bulb. All my eagerness to please was rewarded there. If I behaved well, I got a pat on the head. Studying hard got me a smile and a scrawled red star on the margin of my paper. I loved it and gave it my heart and soul from the very start. School was the answer to home and to the silences there, to my mother's distance and reserve.

No doubt, she was overwhelmed and exhausted. Though she was no longer running a farm, she was still, at the age of thirty, trying to raise four boys, the oldest only seven. Her fifth son, Christopher, had died only a year before under terrible circumstances, and I fear that the move to Rensselaerville was itself my parents' substitute for mourning his death. Add to that the fact that her husband was still completing his medical residency forty miles away. But there may also have been something inherently remote in her temperament. When I try to remember her then, I see her standing in the dark kitchen like a larger tree among that dense sapling thicket that is table and chair legs. She's surrounded by a larger dark but on her shoulders and head there's dappling light like sun on highest leaves. I'm too small to climb her trunk and she's unbending, oblivious, her arms as unreaching, unreachable as distant branches.

In one of the few family photos I have from that time, so much of the story is already there in people's faces and gestures. We're sitting on the back porch in Renssalaerville. I'm hunched between my parents, beaming up at my father worshipfully. He has an anxious, round-faced, diapered Jonathan balanced on his lap and is totally unconscious of me as he smiles his patented smile into the camera. Bill's standing at the outer edge of the group, dark-haired, wearing a desperado's kerchief around his neck and a smirk that's a child's echo of my father's smile, a first indication he's already an apprentice scapegrace.

And then there's my mother holding a blanket-wrapped baby Peter in her arms. She could be a German peasant girl posing for a Madonna and Child, except her smile is enigmatic, Italian. She gazes steadily out, but her look is veiled, withheld, as if some heavenly sadness had settled heavily upon her. And her smile, for all its loveliness, is vague and unearthly; her smile is not meant for anyone on earth.

11

Germantown

THE SUMMER I WAS SIX, MY FATHER FINISHED HIS RESIDENCY and the time came for him to set up as a doctor. While we lived in Alcove, he had met a remarkable woman doctor, Dr. Perkins, who had an office in the nearby village of Westerlo and a practice that extended all through the hills of that area. She had arrived there in the early twenties and been there ever since.

Though I was only five or six when we knew her, I remember her face very clearly: thin and sharp-beaked like a hawk's and with a silvery helmet of hair. Slight yet wiry, she was Joan of Arc transformed from warrior to healer, though in her version Joan lived an unimaginably long and tireless time. She was elderly when I was a small child, but she kept working until the day she died. Many years later, I saw an article from an Albany newspaper celebrating her ninetieth birthday that described how she still charged four dollars for an office visit, five for a house call, and still lived in a window-less room just off her office that contained nothing but a bed, a lamp, and a Bible.

She was a tiny woman, hardly five feet tall. She had such a pres-ence of authority that when people inclined their heads to listen to her, it seemed to me they were bowing out of respect. She so impressed my parents that they named my baby sister after her. And even more than that, her firm example inspired my compassless father to establish a rural practice and spend his life working where doctors were needed most.

So it was that in 1953, having finished his residency in Albany, Dad moved us all to Germantown, to start his own country practice. Germantown was a hamlet in southern Columbia County in the mid–Hudson Valley on the east bank of the river. It had one red light on Route 9G, the main north-south highway that ran from Albany to New York. Down by the Hudson River, there was a train station, but the New York Central had long ceased stopping there. Two or three cement-block structures loomed up over the houses like medieval fortresses over their clustered huts—these were cold-storage buildings for apple and pear crops. The village proper, about a half mile back from the river, consisted of about fifty houses, two grocery stores, a drugstore and a candy and newspaper store, the Central House bar, and a funeral home. In addition, there was a locally owned independent phone company, a small bank, and a brassiere factory that employed ten women. We were too far above New York for there to be any tourism or summer people. Most people were poor, working either as small dairy farmers, fruit growers, or in the cement factory in the nearby city of Hudson.

My parents arrived in Germantown driving a green van of the sort no one drove in those days—a modified panel truck, really. Perfect for a gang of kids, but enough to set the whole town talking, especially alongside the fact that my father did his doctoring in flannel shirts and work boots, not the starched white shirts and bow ties people expected.

Bill and I began attending Germantown Central School, a single brick building midway between the river and the village. Each dawn school buses prowled the dirt roads and long drives of farmhouses for a radius of fifteen miles and still managed to gather only about thirty or so students for each of the twelve grades.

When we first moved to Germantown, we rented briefly in the village, but my parents wanted something with more land and we soon settled in a farmhouse, which we called "the red house," about five miles distant. It stood on a low ridge with fenced pasture on one side and a hay field sloping away toward a shallow, marshy valley on the other. Besides a hay barn, a large garage, a chicken coop, and other outbuildings, it came with about thirty acres of fields and scrub woods. Moving there, my parents could continue to dabble in rural life, raising chickens, haying the fields, eventually gathering a small herd of saddle horses.

It's a daunting task to move into a new town and lure patients away from the old, ignorant doc who's been there for decades, though he's almost senile now, coasting toward reluctant retirement with his drinking catching up to him as he wraps one pink Cadillac after another around fence post or oak. My father worked hard, worked steadily six days a week, would drive out night or day on house calls, gradually memorizing the vast maze of roads and shortcuts, slowly building his practice.

Dad was a good doctor, too; he enjoyed his job, especially in the early days, though later he would say most of general practice was kid's stuff. Most of all, though, he had the gift of healing—people felt better after they saw him. He seemed able to transfer his energy to his ailing patients as easily as he flashed his charming grin. Having been lured into medicine by the dazzle of science, he would never be comfortable with this power that resided as much in his person as in his diagnoses and pills. We kids seldom saw him—he was either gone by the time we got up, or still asleep after having gotten home at eleven or so at night, as he always did.

Once every month or two, we'd all get away across the river to dinner at a tavern named Red's in Coxakie. On these rare family trips, even the minor rituals of connection—like playing the spelling

game "Ghost" as we sipped Cokes and waited for food to come—
were filled with significance and pleasure.

And on the way home, we'd sing "Row, Row, Row Your Boat"
in rounds, or the far more melancholy "Birmingham Jail," whose
haunting refrain I always associate with my mother:

Down in the valley, the valley so low
Hang your head over, hear the wind blow . . .

Having only heard the song aloud, I was never certain whether the
lines were:

Angels in heaven
Know I love you

Or:

Angels in heaven?
No, I love you.

When the singing stopped, I'd stare out the window at the dark
world rushing past and ponder the difference. If it was the former,
then it meant his heart's secrets were open to the eyes of heaven—as
if the angels could look down and see something pure and shining
as a star in the darkness of the human sky. But if it was the latter,
then the depth and intensity of his love was even more impressive—
that he could have preferred his mortal beloved to the perfect beauty
of angels. Such commitment made me think of my parents' upbeat
theme song: "We Belong to a Mutual Admiration Society (My Baby
and Me)."

When the impulse to sing was exhausted, we'd persuade Dad to
tell a story. Almost always, it was "The Monkey's Paw," that tale of
a sailor son who sends home to his parents the gift of a monkey's
severed paw. An accompanying note says the paw has the power to
grant three wishes. When they make their first wish—for a thousand
dollars—the paw opens and closes and immediately the doorbell

rings with a telegram announcing their son has fallen into the ship's engines and been mangled beyond recognition, leaving them his insurance of a thousand dollars. The hysterical mother grabs the paw and demands to see her son again. Just then, another ring at the door. Even as the mother rushes toward the door, the father grabs the paw from her hand and says: "Whatever it is at the door, make it vanish." When the mother flings wide the door there's nothing there but a small pool of oily salt water and blood.

By this time in the story, we were always screaming with terror and glee.

"The Monkey's Paw" scared me with the way it showed how the human heart could trick itself, could want something it thought was good only to be thwarted by something more sinister and powerful in the universe. Or was it all the parents' fault—had their own simple greed undone them? The swiftness with which those three wishes followed each other stunned me, as if at certain crucial moments the world moved too quickly for anyone to understand anything.

12

The Ditch

BEHIND THE RED HOUSE, IN THE DIRECTION OF THE CATSKILL Mountains that marked our western horizon, there was a shallow, swampy valley about three-quarters of a mile wide. After the spring rains and melt, the marsh flooded the lowest corners of our hay field and, during a really wet spring, water might rise up and briefly cover the dirt road that crossed the valley a mile below our house.

Late in my seventh spring, yellow backhoes and bulldozers appeared at the outlet to Bobby Ryder's farm pond, half a mile above our place. All that summer, they chuffed and churned, gouging out a ditch along the line of the small stream that meandered down the valley. Ten feet across, no deeper than three or four feet, the ditch was intended to drain water out of the marsh. As the ditch brimmed, the muskrats sensibly abandoned their cattail mounds in the depleted swamp and took up residence in tunnels dug in the clay banks. And turtles, too, moved down into the ditch.

Soon, that ditch became the landscape of my solitude. Even when I wasn't traipsing its banks on Saturdays and Sundays, I'd travel its length in my imagination, feeling the same delicious shiver one feels tracing a finger along the raised welt of a scar. Sometimes Jon came with me, but usually I was alone. When I walked along the ditch, I had a purpose that held me with the force of obsession. I was in quest of the turtles that sunned themselves on its banks and plopped into the water when they saw me coming. I'd plunge in after to scoop them up, gripping each one by the shell and lifting it up out of the water until it collapsed its clawed feet against its body and pulled in its head with a hiss.

To me, turtles were the strange and silent gods of the ditch. When I caught one, I'd stare for awhile into the colorful impassivity of its face, like a tribesman gazing at the mask of a god or spirit—the bright stripes or patches, the beaked grandeur, the hooded stare of its eyes. There were three species along the ditch. Painted turtles were my favorite—their olive-green shells crisscrossed with wavy ocher lines that mimicked sunlight on a mossy bottom; their underside a glowing orange, and their faces greenish brown streaked with bright yellow and sometimes red like the stylized makeup of characters in Chinese opera.

A spotted turtle had a black, lacquery shell humped like a soldier's helmet and dotted with random yellow spots. Turned over, its bottom was a pumpkin orange, sometimes with a black mottling like archipelagoes on a parchment map.

And then there were the snapping turtles, far larger than the other two species, fierce omnivores with blunt snouts and stubby serrated tails, their moss-grown, irregular shells barely covering clawed feet that were themselves almost lost in rolls of yellow, pimply fat. Snappers were the old gods—chthonic, ugly, and crude—who'd been dethroned by the Olympian gods and locked up in Tartarus. When a snapper attacked, its neck stretched suddenly to two-thirds its body length and what it caught in its jaws it didn't let go. A snapper had no teeth, but its bonelike, eagle's-beak jaw could take your finger off before you knew what happened.

I meant none of the turtles any harm. My task was to catch each one, admire it, scrape the occasional leech from a shell, and then release it again. With my long walking stick which I used to trick snappers to strike so I could reach around and grab them by the tail, I could have been a shepherd following the ditch all day. The turtles became my scattered flock that I must tend and tally—a slender thread of purpose woven through the fabric of pure, joyful wandering in open air where the red-winged blackbirds sent out their three-noted warbles from cattail perches or rose above the marsh with shrill, unconcerned screeches while clouds moved over the valley and wind swayed the reeds and high grasses.

Once, when the surrounding marsh was fairly dry, I made my way through the reeds and up the other side of the valley to explore an old abandoned house. It was almost completely collapsed and empty, but in the basement I discovered the wreck of an old upright piano. Lifted, the warped top revealed the strings still taut and felt-covered hammers—faded green lozenges like individual vertebra from the spinal column of an animal long since rotted.

If I could sit down now at that bedraggled instrument overgrown with wild grapevines, half full of dead leaves, I'd play on it a melody of lost places, of that quiet landscape and the mythic hours of childhood when my brothers and I played hide-and-seek: crouching in the shadow of the chicken coop or standing motionless among the horses by the watering trough; and of dusk seeping from the blue spruce in the front yard until it was dark everywhere and I lay down on my back in the suddenly-cool grass and stared up at the stars and the meandering, summer firefly sparks that drifted among them.

13

House Calls

ONLY ONE THING WAS MORE WONDERFUL THAN THOSE family rides to Coxakie and that was going on house calls alone with my father. There were two options: weekend afternoons or Friday night. The latter was my favorite, because it didn't interfere with playtime and it meant I could stay up late, sometimes until almost midnight (though I would have fallen asleep in the car long before then). It was a privilege Bill and I, as the oldest brothers, vied for. If we both went, it spoiled the whole idea of it, which was to have Dad to yourself. For his part, Dad did his best to discourage us completely: "Look, I'll be out for hours. Nothing but a bunch of house calls. You'll be totally bored."

Always Mom sounded skeptical. Always I had to fight Bill for the privilege. "You went last time. It's my turn." Always it was worth it.

As soon as he could afford it, my father began acquiring a succession of fast, sporty cars—a Plymouth Fury, a Sunbeam Alpine, a Corvette—each of which he drove at calamitous speeds, spewing out huge rooster tails of dust as he raced over the unpaved back roads from patient to patient. It wasn't the speed I loved most, but the fact that once Dad had tucked his black medical bag behind his seat and we'd climbed in, I knew I would have his attention for hours. Often he'd listen to the radio—to the one classical station you could hear that far up the valley—and I'd just relish being with him. But it was even better when I could prod him with a question. Almost any query could ignite long monologues and extended riffs—the gists and piths of a chemically stimulated mind set free on its own associational flows. This was the mid-fifties, and I was just becoming aware of political events and attitudes revolving around the Cold War. All my father needed was my curiosity to get him started:

"What is communism, Dad?"

"Well, Greg, Karl Marx was the founder of communist thinking, and according to him, society should be set up along these lines: 'From each according to his means, to each according to his needs.' In other words, wealth and resources would be distributed in such a way that the poor received more and the rich got less."

"What's wrong with that?" (In the conversations and speeches about communism I'd overheard, there had been no mention at all of any positive ideals.)

"Well, Greg, you have to understand that people seldom live up to ideals. There's a great difference between good ideas and the practical methods used to make them happen. When Lenin became the first communist head of the Soviet Union, he quickly moved to new slogans such as 'The end justifies the means,' and finally 'Might makes right.'"

"That doesn't sound so good," I offered.

"What you saw with Lenin, as with all dictators, is that power corrupts and absolute power corrupts absolutely."

I don't think I really cared about the Cold War and its vicissitudes, but I fell in love with the succinct phrases and maxims my father cobbled together. I didn't know then that they were not his ideas or even his phrasings. From the passenger seat, I gazed up at him, a ten-year-old boy falling under the spell of language and its power to make sense of the world. To me, he was the smartest man who ever lived, the equal of Plato and Kant and the other big thinkers whose tags he'd haul up out of his reading and memory to pour forth in pill-fueled rhapsodies I could only sporadically comprehend.

How brilliant he seemed to me! How in awe of him I was. I was convinced he knew and understood everything. There was no big topic he couldn't reduce to a terse and lucid apothegm that seemed to me like an eagle of the imagination, gliding in a huge, dignified arc over vast landscapes of human experience, only to dive with sudden, murderous force and seize in its talons the heart of some particular issue.

Looking back now, I recognize that his ideas were retrieved from the distant past of his college Western civilization courses, but that doesn't matter. What he was really giving me—the uncontaminated and enduring gift—had to do with language itself. I could feel that he loved the power and beauty of words rhythmically compressed into meaning. He passed that awe on to me, and it's sustained me my whole life.

Despite our shared excitement about ideas and language, my father and I were antipodal temperaments who could only briefly be at peace. House calls provided one of those rare instances of mutual harmony between us. Instead of enduring the boredom of long drives alone, my father was able to indulge his intellectual vanity by unfolding long, abstract discourses to an enthralled listener. And snug in my bucket seat, I basked in my own importance—I was the one who had set him going on these exhilarating riffs. Between one dark farmhouse and the next, there were long intervals as we zoomed over the winding roads. It was easy then, as I listened to my father's voice, to imagine that the world was comprehensible and could be brought within the compass of a single mind expressing itself effort-lessly in sonorous phrases.

14

Bottles

IN A DREAM LAST NIGHT I WAS DIGGING IN MUDDY EARTH and rubble and found a silver coin with the head of a Roman empress, but somehow I knew it was my mother's face, the features worn smooth yet still discernible. I rubbed it until it was clean, until it grew warm in my hand.

It reminded me that, besides country furniture bought at farm auctions up and down the Hudson Valley, my mother also collected antique bottles. On my various solitary wanderings in the woods around the red house, I'd sometimes come on a spot where a farmer, years before there was a town dump, had hauled his trash. Usually some large, unidentifiable object rusting among the trees marked the spot. Or I might actually find the cellar hole of a house long gone and vanished from anyone's memory.

When I found such a place, I'd dig down with a stick or my bare hands, rummaging about in the humus for any bit of buried glass that, unearthed, might be a whole bottle. I must have looked odd, on my hands and knees scrabbling through the leaves in the middle of the woods, like a squirrel searching for fallen nuts. My fingers still remember the sensation of peeling back the strata of hickory leaves—the top layers light brown and dry and lifting off in large patches like bandages, then each successive deeper layer darker and more compressed, the leaves now fragmented and finally wet and cold and traced through with white and yellow threads of mold. And every once in a while, the gritty feel of ancient iron where a can has become nothing but a filigreed bracelet of rust.

Often I'd find the remnants of the metal teapots popular on farms at the turn of the century—a white-speckled gray like guinea hen feathers. And many patent medicine bottles, whole earth-hue rainbows of greens and browns and ambers. The cobalt blue of Phillips' Milk of Magnesia seemed especially magical to my child's eyes, though after I'd brought a few home as trophies, I began to grow more sophisticated under my mother's instruction. Soon, I was holding each find up to the sunlight, searching for the varying thickness of walls or bottoms or trapped air bubbles—any irregularities that might show it was handblown rather than merely poured in a mold. Once I discovered a dark-green bottle with an ingenious stopper—a glass marble resting inside the neck in such a way that when you tipped to pour, it rolled forward and out of the way of the gushing fluid, and then when the bottle was turned upright again, the marble dropped back to cover the opening.

What I found I took home to her—a way of trying to please her, whose love I was so unsure of. I'd watch her wash them in the sink and place them in rows along windowsills, where they glowed brightly. That was the idea, that was my own vague longing: to be lifted up out of the earth into the light.

15

Books

WHEN I WAS ELEVEN AND HOME SICK WITH A COLD, I began reading *The Viking Portable Poe,* a book I'd chosen from our library for its flashy purple cover. In the middle of the afternoon, I ran into the living room where Mom was ironing and told her I'd figured out who was doing the gruesome killings in "The Murders in the Rue Morgue" long before the author himself revealed the secret. She seemed rather thoughtful at this announcement, as I had hoped she'd be. I dearly wanted to impress her with my detective skills though now I suspect it was my ambitious reading choice that struck her. Soon after that she brought me her own two favorite books to read. Her act of entrusting me with her favorite books, of even telling me what her favorite books were, gave me a feeling of exquisite intimacy. By reading these books, I could hope to be close to her in ways that were impossible in the constricted emotional world of our daily family life.

Yet it proved, because of the books themselves—Sigrid Undset's *Kristin Lavransdatter* and Emily Brontë's *Wuthering Heights*—oddly otherwise. I'm eager to celebrate here the fact that her favorite writers were women—Isak Dinesen was another. But I hasten to add that a mother's gift of these two particular books to her shy, inhibited son was a gesture that might have made Freud shudder. That the main characters were women was fine, but these women lived tortuous lives, lives of enormous anguish and oppression. *Kristin Lavransdatter* lay on my heart like a heavy and peculiar stone—a boulder carved with Nordic runes. The story, set in the dismal Middle Ages in Scandinavia, was a historically accurate and tediously exhaustive account of life in that bleak, brutal world of cold and snow and winter days that saw only an hour or so of feeble sun. In my memory, the young heroine was dragged into frozen roadside bushes on one of those endless nights and raped, perhaps by the taciturn man who later became her husband.

I was much too young for this. I hadn't a clue as to the sexual nature of human beings, let alone the mechanics of the enterprise. From what I could gather, it was dark and violent and made the woman feel bad. There wasn't much I could do with that story, nor with Kathy's agonies in *Wuthering Heights*. Now, belatedly, I see those novels as reflections of my mother's inner life—she, like their heroines, was a woman of enormous intelligence, passion, and longing, but all of it thwarted and tangled up in a world where men held the real power.

What had at first seemed a great gift from my mother, a gesture of affection and identification with me, turned into a grim burden. I desperately craved her approval, wanted to read and love her favorite books. But they took me far from that easy connection to female being that had been mine in third grade when Sherry Oswald, the leader of the girls, announced to all and sundry on the playground that I and only I among the boys could play with them, because I wasn't rough or mean.

When you open a book's covers you create a white ravine only a few inches across, but these books of my mother's widened and deepened into a sheer chasm with boys and men on one side, girls and women on the other. I felt myself caught on a frail, swaying bridge suspended between them, unsure which way I was supposed to go.

Now, I see my mother's books as messages from another world. My father was fascinated by ideas and power and politics, and he offered me his wisdom in terse sayings that perfectly mirrored his detachment from people and their daily concerns. My mother believed in another world—a world of particular, individual personalities embedded in landscapes and circumstances, often even mired in them. Hers was not the world of omnipotent philosophers and statesmen, but of vulnerable creatures at the mercy of forces beyond their control. Prominent among those destructive forces were the characters' own emotions. Their unlived and unexpressed lives were turbulent and inconsolable and filled with emotions intense as whirlpools that sucked them down to ruin and death.

16

New Heights

BESIDES HOUSE CALLS, THE ONLY WAY OF BEING WITH DAD involved signing on for some adventure he was organizing. Going on house calls was palpably safer, once you discounted his notoriously fast driving, because his chemical energy was mostly verbal then. His adventures, on the other hand, often had a pronounced element of physical risk. And under the influence of amphetamine, my father's sense of confidence easily slipped over into arrogance and grandiosity. A cheerful recklessness possessed him and with it he'd incite and cajole his children to join him.

When I was eleven, he was determined to build his own transmitting tower for the two-way radio he'd installed in his car to receive messages during his long house call odysseys. The tower was unloaded off a flatbed as half a dozen eight-foot, triangular sections of tubular metal. Once the base section had been set in concrete, you attached one to the next until the tower rose to its full forty-eight-foot height. To do this, you had to climb to the top of whatever section was completed, hoist the next section up with a thick rope and then wrestle it into a precarious balance above you until you could bolt it in place. Every twenty feet, you ran woven steel support cables down from each corner to the ground. Dad's enthusiasm alone couldn't construct this tower, so Bill and I were recruited to help. Once we were up past thirty feet, it was terrifying. There was something naked and skeletal about this structure— a tree branch is alive under your hand but these metal rungs had the smooth chill of polished gravestones. As you climbed it, each step or accidental bang of your wrench sent a thin shudder through the tower's whole dead length. Half the fun of climbing a tree is being welcomed into the lushness of it, absorbed and concealed in its generous, living foliage. Strapped to the tower by a leather safety belt, I felt vulnerable and exposed like a bear who's clambered awkwardly up a barkless, branchless trunk that, rotten and hollow, could topple at any moment. Still, as the tower neared its full height, it was amazing to see the domestic landscape I knew so well transformed—the slate tiles of the house and even the barn's rusting tin roof below me and the forest canopy stretching away level with my eyes and flat as a plain with here and there the hillock of a giant oak or hickory.

I had such confidence in my father that he could easily persuade me to go along on any adventure, no matter how scary. When Bill and Jon declined his invitation to go rock climbing, that made it all the more appealing from my point of view: less competition, more opportunities to prove myself.

Dad hadn't climbed since his college days, when he and some Columbia buddies had scaled the Palisades. Anecdotes from that happy-go-lucky and beer-powered adventure filled the thirty-mile drive we made down toward Bear Mountain one June weekend. Our goal was a cliff called Breakneck Ridge on the east bank of the Hudson. We had ropes, pitons, and rock hammers—all the appropriate equipment. It didn't seem to bother Dad that I had never rock-climbed before or that I was only a scrawny eleven-year-old.

Miles from any other habitation, we pulled into the gravel parking lot of a tavern whose huge, green-shingled roof made it seem like a moss-covered boulder rolled off the mountains. Hoisting our coil of rope, rucksacks, and canteens, we followed a short path through thick woods that stopped abruptly where the talus rose in a steep slope right out of the tree trunks. Once we'd clambered up over the loose stone, we stood in a little pool of morning sun at the base of the cliff with the face proper rising a hundred feet above us the shape and mottled-gray color of a sperm whale's forehead. The rope Dad tied between us was pale and stiff, an ivory umbilicus bristly with strands of hemp itchy as tiny wires against my palms. After he had hooked the pitons and hammer to his belt, we surveyed the rock and planned our ascent. Dad took the lead, showing me how to face spread-eagled into the cliff—how, if I held myself flat and splayed against the rock, the tiniest handhold could steady me, the narrowest ledges could take my full weight. Everything went fine for the first hour. We worked our way up and along generous ledges with plenty of handhold, and then, more slowly, with pitons pounded into the rock, moved obliquely out over the vertical face itself. But something went wrong somewhere—we got as far up as we could go, at least seventy feet, but it wasn't the top.

It was then that I learned a basic climbing lesson—how much easier the way up is than the way down. As I looked back and to the side, I could see no trace of the route we'd come by. Ledges that seemed obvious and spacious during our ascent had now vanished entirely from my terrified sight. Before I knew it, I was dangling at the end of my climbing rope like a scared, skinny spider at the tip of his thread as my father swung me back and forth—slow pendulum—until at last I could scramble onto a ledge far over to one side where the ledges were wider and closer together and it was possible to edge my way down.

On our walk back to the car, he was uncharacteristically silent, while I chattered a nonstop nervous celebration of the miracle of solid, underfoot earth where one could run or dance in any direction without fear of falling. My father used the drive home to convince me we were never in any real danger, and by the time we arrived he was ready to refashion the whole day into a certified Orr adventure. With humorous, exaggerated gestures, our serious misadventure on a vertical cliff became a mock-heroic yarn emphasizing his resourcefulness in the face of astonishing and inexplicable complications. I, too, was given a role in this tale, one intended to make my brothers green with envy. My father was like a wily rug merchant who, with a single dramatic gesture, unsnaps a bright carpet that settles definitively over the plain bare fact of the wood floor. But this time his glibness didn't fool me, though I watched in fascination as my brothers, in their innocence and ignorance, were taken in. No narrative, no matter how cleverly fashioned and unfolded, could supplant certain basic sensations I'd felt that morning: the bump, slide, and push as I struggled desperately to control my relentless swing back and forth across the cliff; the terrifying sense of nothing but air beneath my feet and warm, rough rock inches from my face, scraping my palms raw.

17

The *Chiron*

OFTEN MY FATHER'S ILL-ADVISED ADVENTURES INVOLVED
the whole family. They would begin with high spirits and enthusiasm, only to gradually lose their hopeful momentum and finally
seem to yield to a secret and powerful attraction to chaos. For one
of Dad's rare, brief vacations, we rented a sailboat on Long Island
Sound. A few days before we left, he brought home six neon-yellow,
hooded sweatshirts—one for each of us except baby Nancy. With a
black Magic Marker, he customized each with an individual voyage
name. Bill, who was thirteen, was vociferous in his opposition to
the trip and the whole idea of family togetherness. These outbursts
earned him the nickname "SHANGHAIED," which Dad prompt-
ly inscribed above a pair of handcuffs across the back of his sweatshirt. I wish I could remember my own sea name, or Jon's or
Peter's—they might give a hint of how my father saw us, at least in
that moment. But my gaze was mostly forward, taking in the complex dynamics between Bill and my parents as if I might, from all
his misbehavior and grumbling, gain clues about how to insinuate
myself into their good graces. And so I see so clearly my father
spreading his own sweatshirt out on the kitchen table and inking

"ODYSSEUS" in large black letters across its bright yellow surface.

He was then at the height of his fascination with Nikos Kazantzakis, the author of *Zorba the Greek* and other works. Though my father lacked all powers of introspection, he knew himself well enough to see he had none of Zorba's peasant sensuality or earthy exuberance. On the other hand, he was gripped by an intense identification with Odysseus in Kazantzakis' epic *The Odyssey: A Modern Sequel*, which picks up where Homer left off, with its hero embarking alone from Ithaka on new adventures and sexual escapades. Profoundly restless, endlessly eager to test his wits and strength against ever new challenges: this was Kazantzakis's Odysseus, and it was also my father's larger-than-life dream of himself. To be forever leaving a shore or a person without a backward glance. Odysseus in his swift ship, my father each year in a new, fast car racing over the back roads of Columbia County. And to be a hero—to be ever vigilant for the next threat or challenge—is also to be absolved of the past, which no longer matters, is no longer real. Granted, Odysseus might entertain people with tales of his past travails (some of them true, some not), but everything was on his own terms. He didn't answer to anyone, even his wife or son.

Yet, for all his restlessness, my father needed a stable counterpart, someone whose very stasis would make it possible to measure the hero's brave wanderings, and so my father decorated my mother's yellow sweatshirt with the name "PENELOPE." In the version of that story my parents acted out, Penelope was not physically abandoned; her fate may have been worse, it was certainly more complex. She was condemned to accompany her wayward husband —to be applauding audience or appalled witness—to be near him, yet always far away.

We arrived at a City Island marina late one afternoon to board the *Chiron*, the thirty-foot sloop we were renting. Unfortunately, by the time we'd loaded provisions and were ready to leave harbor, "Small Craft Warning" pennants were flying from the marina flagstaff, and the Coast Guard radio was ordering all pleasure craft to get off the water before a line of squalls hit. It is dusk. We watch all the boats converging toward their respective harbors, hull to hull in their haste like white ants trying to get through the same few entrances to the safety of their nest. All except us. As the rest of the boats, Chriscraft and cruisers and daysailers, as far as the eye could see, swarmed back to shore, we alone motored out into the channel, and then, reaching the wider waters of the sound itself, hoisted sail as the wind kicked up and the waves turned to whitecaps in the growing dark.

People sleep at night. Small boats don't go out at twilight into unknown waters and fierce, predicted storms. No father, who is himself the single competent sailor aboard, would head to sea in the dark under such conditions with a wife, four little kids, and a baby. No sane father would do such a thing. And yet, in his own arrogant, amphetamine-addled mind it all made sense to my father. Why should he waste his precious vacation sitting in harbor while the storm blew out, when he could easily take the boat straight down the sound—right through the storm and out the other side? Or maybe he meant to outrun it.

Whatever his plan, what the rest of us experienced was a terrifying night of rain and racing seas and winds howling in the rigging. The sea was so rough everyone but Dad and me went below to huddle and puke in the bunks. Dad gripped the helm the whole, unrelenting night, fighting the winds and keeping clear of land as best he could though the waves were too high to see shore beacons or landmarks. I lay wedged and white-faced in a corner of the open cockpit, soaked through but too frightened to move. Wrapped in a blanket and braced against the shudder and crash of waves, I stared all night at my father's face. Barely two yards away, it often seemed ghostly and vague as a fog-veiled moon. The less distinct it was, the more intently I stared, as if my gaze might burn through the haze and add to his dwindling reserves what force of will I possessed. Other times, I simply watched for the slightest hint that the inevitable disaster was at last upon us, as if even the least forewarning would be better than none at all.

And then, slowly, the gray of predawn began to slip under the low roof of storm clouds and I could see clearly his grim, exhausted, triumphant face. By dawn, everything had gone according to his plan—the storm had dispersed and under a strong but steady breeze we rounded the northern point of Long Island, passing through Orient Race to anchor safely at Northport. What a victory! Only hours into our vacation and already, according to him, our adventure was well under way. My mother was faint with her praise for his sailing skills, but she had been fainter still with protests that might have kept us safe in harbor the previous night.

We moored that whole day in Northport. Perhaps Dad was exhausted; perhaps we all mutinied at another day on the water. The following day, we sailed east toward Block Island off the coast of Rhode Island. Our route took us across the channel used by the Atlantic Submarine Fleet as it entered and departed its home base on the Connecticut shore. By the craziest of coincidences, we were sailing across that channel at exactly the time that four of the submarines were steaming along the surface in a line headed out to sea. I'd never seen a real submarine before. The ones I'd seen in World War II movies like *Run Silent, Run Deep* were slender and graceful, with an elaborate fretwork of antennae on their conning towers. These that steamed toward us now were a new generation: gigantic and round-bodied, their conning towers stripped down and hydrodynamic like the dorsal fins of huge sea creatures. Their scale and sleekness made them seem alive yet impersonal, as if they were somehow beyond human control like Leviathan in the book of Job.

"A ship under sail always has the right of way over a ship under power," my father announced aloud in a quietly belligerent tone.

We stared at him, dumbfounded that he intended to keep course straight on between these sinister giants. As if a line of elephants would swerve for an ant! It provided a rare chance to see my father's craziness through outside eyes: I craned my neck up to where a sub loomed above us so close I could see the frown on the officer's face as he stared down from the high conning tower at our toy boat bobbing in his wake.

Part Three

Part Three

18

After

WHEN SOMEONE YOU LOVE DIES SUDDENLY, THE PROCESS of surviving them is complex. Part of the difficulty is separating out your entangled identities. Grieving, you celebrate the love bond between you and the dead one, but also, as you grieve, you are distinguishing yourself from the dead one.

Whenever I thought of Peter, my feelings were so tangled up in guilt that I, too, wanted to be dead. And I thought of him constantly in those days and weeks and months after his death.

When I imagine healthy grieving, I see the living one packing a little boat with clothes and food and mementos. The dead one climbs into the boat and when the time for departure comes, you send him on his voyage into his new life. You, the living, stand on the shore and watch as the lost loved one rows out into the dark alone.

No one spoke to me about Peter's dying. No one told me how to help my little brother on his journey to the land of the dead; no one showed me how to bless him and let him go. No one offered to help me sort out the threads of memory and guilt and grief that confused our two identities into a single tangle. I did my best. It felt as if I sat for hours on the floor of my room, trying to separate out our two selves, but I could not—it was hopeless. And so I gave up and thrust the whole snarl back inside my body, back through my own wound that had opened when Peter died. From then on, Peter and I were inextricable in my thoughts. He became a part of me and lived inside me more intimately mingled than warp and woof of the same cloth, basic and mysterious as the place where the pale blue of veins meets the scarlet of arteries.

19

Returning

WAS IT ONLY A WEEK SINCE PETER HAD DIED? AND HERE WE were, Bill, Jon, and me, waiting by the old shed at the driveway's end, stamping our feet and sending up great clouds of breath as if we were pastured horses trying to keep warm in mid-November. And then the whining of gears as the empty school bus labored up the hill toward us. Was it possible that everything would go on the same, though one of us had vanished entirely? Nothing seemed different—the heavy hiss and clack of the opening doors sounded as it always had; the thump of our feet on the three high steps up and then the sudden, clear, desolate view of the vacant green seats on either side of the aisle. First on in the morning, last off at night—we Orr kids had our choice of seats for the forty-minute ride to school. I slumped into the back row by the emergency door. From there I hoped to control the whispering and the furtive, curious glances over seat backs, thought I could hold them at bay. But I couldn't, and I stared instead out the window as the bleak landscape unrolled —the trees now leafless and skeletal, except the oaks still wrapped in their brown tatters; in the fields, sumac thickets lifting their torches of withered berries, the tall grasses gone dry and pale so the only green hugged the frosty ground or brightened as watercress at the edges of pasture streams. As our bus turned in farmyard driveways, Holsteins clustered in the lee of the barn, hock-deep in muck, gazed up with mournful vacancy. Nothing was different; nothing unexpected.

Soon enough, too soon, we were on the road into town and then pulling into the oval parking lot where the other buses, each its own distinctively faded shade of orange or yellow, were gathered like old carp at the edge of an autumn pool.

Somehow I managed to get through the halls full of kids shouting and banging their lockers; managed to get to my seventh-grade homeroom and to my desk. I was among kids I'd known my whole life. They looked the same as they did a week ago; probably I did too. But those I tried to look in the face shifted their eyes away, while I felt everyone behind me staring intently. The invisible pillar of shame that had protected me during the funeral had disappeared now. I could hear and see everything. What was worse, I could feel. Nothing stood between me and my wretchedness. So I hid my face in my arms on my desk, the way I used to in grade school when I was exhausted and wanted to nap. If the mark of Cain was stamped on my forehead, all I could do was hide my face to conceal it. It felt good and safe to have my eyes pressed into the dark crook of my elbow and to feel the polished smoothness of the desktop cool against my chin. I stayed there the whole time of homeroom, but when the bell rang for classes to begin, I couldn't get up. I heard the clatter of chairs thrown back, the sliding together of hoisted books, the shuffle of feet toward the door, and the slamming open of the door itself as everyone hurried out. I heard everything, but I didn't move. I didn't want to move, but even if I had wanted to, I wouldn't have been able with the weight of all my shame pressing down on me, holding my face against the desk.

After all my classmates had left, and she saw that I wasn't going to get up, Mrs. Hawes asked me if I wanted to go with her to the office. Jon was already there, sitting in a chair outside the principal's door. I saw that his feet didn't even reach the floor; I saw he was weeping quietly and staring at his knees.

20

A Dream

IN THE DREAM, I'M STANDING WITH MY CLASSMATES AND friends in the lunch line that winds its way out through the cafeteria doors and along the corridor as far as the stairs to the gym. It's the most social time in the whole school day—when we clown quietly or lean against the concrete-block wall painted a pale green enamel and talk about everything that connects us in a superficial yet real way: sports and the difficulties of homework or an impending test, movies or what we saw on TV last night. Suddenly, I'm aware that crutches have appeared under me and are propping me up— I feel the awkward pressure of rubber guards in my armpits and my hands wrapped around smooth wood grips at my sides as I struggle to keep my balance. Looking down I discover that below my waist I'm only octopus tentacles dangling to the linoleum floor in a gray, snaky confusion of suckers and rubbery, slimy flesh. I can't tell which is worse—my own grotesque transformation or my friends' faces shocked wide with horror and disgust.

21

The Old House

WHEN I WAS ELEVEN, THE YEAR BEFORE PETER'S DEATH, WE moved to what we called "the old house." It was another ten miles further from Germantown than the red house, and the nearest neighbors with kids our age were more than a mile away. My mother's two closest friends lived in Germantown, a full half-hour's drive over small, winding roads. My father had no friends, neither then nor later. His ready grin and charm were part of his professional persona, but he never trusted or let anyone close. Perhaps there was also an element of intellectual and social snobbery in his aloofness. There were few people in our area who had gone to college. Even the teachers at Germantown Central School, some of whom were my mother's friends, had only graduated from state teacher's colleges.

The lack-luck farmer from whom my parents bought the old house kept his goats and a pig in the dirt-floored front hall. The plaster walls were dark with the residue of decades of greasy smoke. It took a visionary eye to see the house's possibilities; there was no historical marker by the driveway to point you beyond its decrepit present state into its interesting past.

The twenty-foot-square main room had been built with enormously thick stone walls and functioned, when needed, as a fort where Dutch settlers could take refuge in the late seventeenth century. From there, it had expanded incrementally as farmhouses do when the farm prospers—more rooms and a low second story were added, though none in at least a century. To rescue a house this unusual intrigued both my parents and so they bought it, though before we could move in, the whole house had to be dismantled and rebuilt again, the three chimneys taken right down to the ground. Many of the beams had to be replaced, and the whole structure scrutinized and stabilized. Despite all this restoration, and the installation of electric heat panels along walls and below windows, it was never a warm house and in winter it could be freezing.

My room was directly above the stone fort. All the bedrooms opened out into a central upstairs hall where a balcony ran around three sides and on the fourth a staircase descended to the main entranceway. A chimney rose up on the fourth side so that the staircase was actually a double staircase—one set of stairs descending on either side of the chimney. Words like "balconied hall" and "double staircase" imply something rather grand and imposing, but in fact it was a squat, low-ceilinged pioneer farmhouse in a cold valley. The scale of the rooms gave a feeling of stuffy closeness rather than intimacy. And finally and above all, the house was dark. No matter how many times I opened my bedroom door in the morning, I was always a bit shocked by the gloom of the central hall.

Such a house seemed designed to encourage each of us to close the door again, to retreat back into his or her own room. And after Peter's death, there was all the more motive to do so.

My parents' bedroom was large, with a pressed-tin ceiling and a view down over the lawn to the stream that flowed behind our house. They shared the room, though, by then, I doubt they shared much else. What they said and felt in the months after Peter's death is a mystery to me. Did they speak of it at all, or did they respond by returning to the painful silence that followed Christopher's death? If they spoke, was it to blame themselves or each other?

About four months after Peter's death, I awoke in the middle of the night to a high screeching sound, followed by short, staccato screams. We got out of our beds and gathered in the dark hall outside my parents' bedroom door. My mother crouched down at the doorsill in her white cotton nightgown, hugging her knees like a child, sobbing and rocking back and forth.

"Mom, what's wrong?" Bill asked.

"Your father doesn't love me anymore! He wants to leave."

Who could imagine such a thing? Their door was open enough for us to see into the lighted room where my father stood, silently watching us, fully dressed. It was as if his being dressed there, then, in the middle of the night, was a kind of confirmation of his intention to leave right then. As if he was ready to walk out at that moment and not come back. That was the way the horrors of reality had become for us: sudden and absolute, arriving with no warning. Everything you knew and believed changed completely in an instant.

"He wants to leave us. He doesn't love me anymore."

Mom kept repeating these phrases and pressing her face against her knees.

"Barbara, calm down," my father said from where he stood. His voice was steady and flat as if he were taking charge of an animal too agitated to understand his words but that could be controlled by a tone of voice. My mother kept sobbing, not responding to him or looking up at us. Bill, Jon, Nancy, and I stood in a semicircle around her in the dark hall, not knowing what to do, not even comprehending what she was saying, dumbfounded to hear our mother who was always so calm and invulnerable moaning inconsolably like a small child.

My father was standing at the door now, holding it open.

"Barbara, get a hold of yourself. Kids, get back to your rooms."

He opened the door wider. Mom got unsteadily to her feet, went back inside, and my father closed the door. We were too shocked and frightened to dare open it again. What happened next? Did Dad sleep on a couch that night? Did Mom sleep at all? We must, at some point, have returned to our own rooms. We could not have stood all night in the cold of a dark hall. The intensity of such moments is unsustainable. But how did we, having witnessed our whole world torn into pieces, turn calmly back to our separate rooms? How did we climb into beds that had already long forgotten the heat of our bodies? How did we turn out the lights and go back to sleep?

And soon Dad was moving out. Was gone.

He moved into a room in his mother's small house. She lived twenty miles away, in Germantown proper where Dad's town office was. We kids didn't see him for several months after that. An even deeper gloom and silence settled over the old house. Mom spent hours in her room. When she emerged, we'd scan her face anxiously. She was red-eyed from crying, but she wouldn't talk about how she felt or show her suffering in front of us. We did our best to cope. Bill closed himself up in his room and listened to records or the radio; his whole life, music would be his consolation and escape. Jon and I whispered together, trying to understand what was going on. Peter's death, for all its horror, was explicable: a gun went off, a bullet entered a child's skull, and he died. Of course, what was incomprehensible to me about Peter's death was why he had to die and why I killed him. But the story of Cain offered me a painful refuge: I was the bad brother who slew his good sibling. But how could we comprehend our parents' separation? We had never seen or even heard of families splitting up. I knew a fair number of kids whose parents fought and argued; I'd witnessed one or two cruel squabbles between man and wife at one of my friend's houses. I'd even seen Mom cry once in front of us: at the table at the red house, three years before, she'd burst into tears. We had been utterly baffled. After dinner that night, my parents and the rest of us had gone for a walk along our dirt road and my father had said calming things I've long since forgotten. But we never knew then what it was that had made her so upset—she kept that in, and we were grateful to let something so mysterious and disturbing pass out of memory. Now, everyone in Germantown soon knew my father had moved out of the house, so the painful mystery of his leaving acquired whole layers of social shame.

When summer arrived, Mom drove Jonathan and me up the valley to stay with a family she knew, the Chalmers. They ran a goat dairy farm in Castleton, on the river not far below Albany. Mom had met them back in the days of the Alcove farm when they rented milking goats Mom was raising. Tom Chalmer, the patriarch, was a large charismatic man with deep-set eyes, a gravelly voice, and huge hands. He, his wife, and their two grown, unmarried daughters ran the largest goat dairy in the eastern part of the state. It was a serious business and a busy place, so Jon and I were soon put to work. We helped ready the milking machines at dawn, lead in the full-uddered goats, lug the brimming stainless steel milk cans here and there by their double handles, hose down the milking room, and feed the baby goats their medicines. How grateful we were to be caught up in the excitement of something new and to forget the misery and confusion of what was going on at home. How grateful to be transported to this world with its ceaseless, urgent structure, loading stacks of bright orange caps into the bottling machine or starting each goat with a hand-squeezed stream before hooking her to the milker's black rubber cups. And best of all, there were the kids to care for—the dozen or so baby goats who were so energetic and playful, always prancing or racing in circles, or butting heads and then springing on all four feet at once to this or that side at hilarious angles. It seemed impossible that such spontaneous, exuberant creatures could grow into the stolid, dull-faced adults who spent their whole day with their muzzles face down in the pasture grass.

Inevitably, though Tom informed us we were "responsible" for the whole herd of kids, Jon and I each chose and named our own particular favorites. Mine had tan flanks, a black streak down its spine and three colors—tan, buff, and black—meeting in a mask at its snout. Jon's was white as a snowball. It was our bad luck that one of our chosen kids died of an infection in the short time we were there. I don't remember if it was Jon's goat or mine. I do remember the two of us weeping in a huddle on the brown tiles of the milk house floor, and Tom at first looming over us like a huge shadow, then crouching down to deliver a deep-voiced commentary on the harsh world of nature and the perils of placing your heart there.

Then our time at the farm was over. Driving us back to the old house, Tom spoke for the first time about the topic we had all avoided.

"You know, you kids are lucky. Your folks are wonderful people."

Jon and I were sitting, silent and disconsolate, in the back of his old green Dodge as he drove down Route 9G toward Germantown. I could see his powerful eyes in the rearview mirror, fixing us steadily, as if he had no need to pay attention to the highway. With that deep, gruff voice and those eyes framed in the flat oval of the mirror as though they were floating in the air, it could have been one of God's harsher angels talking. Maybe this was the voice of the cherubim with the flaming sword that Adam and Eve heard when they circled back and tried to sneak into Eden again. A voice both infinitely authoritative and insane with simplicity of mission. Did he think we didn't know our parents were wonderful? That wasn't our problem. We were struggling with what kids always struggle with: how had we caused this disaster? And in my case, I already knew. I had caused it by killing Peter. A story simple and biblical; something a twelve-year-old could comprehend.

"Your mom's going to need you kids to be strong now. This is a rough time for her."

Tom knew about strength; he seemed to Jon and me to be the epitome of it.

"We'll try," I ventured timidly.

"You're going to have to do more than try. You've got to be tough. No whining. That sort of thing won't help at all. I'm counting on you."

His eyes returned to the road.

The next day, our whole, regrouped family climbed into Mom's Chevy station wagon and drove down to meet Dad at a marina further down the Hudson. While Jon and I had been away, Dad had bought a sailboat—an eighteen-foot daysailer with a small covered cabin. He'd traveled to the boatyard on Long Island to pick it up and sailed it by himself back up the Hudson. We hadn't seen him in months. I ran full tilt toward him, down the riverbank and out onto the small wooden marina dock with the hollow thump of my soles slapping down and the floating dock giving way under my weight in a sway and counter-sway that surprised my balance and almost made me stagger and fall. Hugging him, I felt the wiry stubble of beard with which he always celebrated his brief vacations. Despite the thick black stubble, his lower cheeks were sunburned below the line of the khaki Navy cap that he wore with the brim turned down. We all stood on the dock awhile, admiring the boat, then set out on the river for a sail.

There was no wind so we motored across the flat river toward Peekskill to gaze close up at the marvel of the mothball fleet at anchor in a large cove: row after row of huge, gray Liberty ships chained together as they had been since the end of the Second World War. Minimally maintained, their engines packed in grease, their bow chains weeping rust streaks toward the water, a hundred cargo ships waited quietly in their bay for a summons to some new war.

As we motored quietly among their looming shapes—the top of our mast not even rising a third of the way up their hulls—my father told us that things weren't going well for him.

"You think these boats are big. When I was sailing through New York harbor, I passed an empty cargo boat riding so high out of the water that half its giant propeller was exposed. I thought of maneuvering my boat up close to it, so I could get wrecked by the propeller and you could collect the insurance money and be rid of me, but I wasn't sure I could make it look like an accident."

We stared at him in appalled silence.

Maybe my mother was as naive as her children, I don't know. Maybe none of us realized how self-dramatizing and manipulative my father was to impose his fantasy on us. Maybe even he, deep in his narcissistic anguish, wasn't aware of what he was saying and how it would affect us. What I felt then was the horrible threat that my father, too, might be taken violently and permanently from me.

No doubt Dad told us many other things that day—after all, we hadn't seen him in months and despite the apparent serenity of his sailor's squint, he was probably high on amphetamine as well—but that's all I remember. That and the sun on the river, the boat rocking in the small chop as it made its slow way among the ghostly hulls.

22

Visitors

AFTER THAT MIDSUMMER DAY OF SAILING UNDER THE BOWS and fantails of the mothball fleet, we didn't see Dad again for several weeks.

Then Jon, Bill, and I were invited to meet him for a sail in Catskill where he'd docked the boat. Early one Saturday afternoon, Mom dropped us at the small marina and drove off. We greeted Dad with a kind of awkward joy and went aboard, but then we didn't leave right away. Dad was dawdling, delaying our departure. A light blue Volkswagen pulled up onto the cinders at the foot of the dock, and a young woman named Inga Klemmer got out and came toward Dad with a big smile.

We knew her slightly, having met her three years before, when we lived at the red house and she was fifteen or sixteen. She was the daughter of one of Dad's patients, a German-Swiss immigrant who lived briefly in a village near Germantown, then moved to the nearby city of Hudson. Inga's father was a violent, abusive alcoholic who had finally abandoned his family. We didn't usually learn gossip about Dad's patients, but he'd told us these things because he had decided, out of sympathy for the Klemmers, to invite Inga and her brother to visit our house and ride our horses.

When we moved to the red house, my parents had become interested in riding, or, more likely, Dad had gotten excited about it and brought the rest of us along. Over the course of several years, he'd assembled a herd of six or seven horses from buys here and there—usually in the fall when the two or three seedy nags kept by a kid's summer camp were no longer worth the hay it would take to feed them through the winter. Such horses would be headed to the dogfood factory, or else the owner might call Doc Orr, who for fifty or a hundred dollars apiece, would buy them and thus save the trucking fee to the Albany slaughterhouse.

Not all our horses were at the ragged end of their lives. My father's horse, Pogo, was a fine, sleek quarterhorse and my father had a correspondingly lovely Western saddle for him. My mother's horse was placid and healthy, though a little too fond of windfall apples. In her eagerness to browse them, she'd once dashed under a low-branched tree and knocked my mother out of her saddle in the sixth month of her pregnancy with Nancy, breaking Mom's hip and sending her to the hospital. All this, as Grammie Howe once told me, despite the fact that doctors told Mom she had no business riding at all, since she had a heart condition left over from childhood rheumatic fever.

My own horse, Pepper, was a spirited and compact beast whose soul, though a bit devilish, moved with my own whenever I galloped her across a field. Lenny was a good, long-legged saddle horse Jon rode; Sneaky Pete, Bill's horse, was not to be trusted, especially during saddling when he'd arch his neck back to nip, then, as you turned to slap his muzzle, surprise you with a pawing kick from his hind leg.

In those days, on weekend mornings, our family might go for a long ride up the dirt road and then through neighbors' orchards and across fields. It was one more way family adventures bound us Orrs into the story of our specialness. We did what other people didn't do. It had something to do with economics—that we could afford to do things others couldn't. But it operated outside social and economic class also. We never joined the country club the few well-to-do local families put together—my father despised the idea, perhaps out of snobbery, since his own father had been on the admissions committee of the Century Club in New York City when Dad was an adolescent. Mostly, we kept to ourselves—as emotionally and socially isolated as we were geographically. We existed in our own, secretly superior world defined in part by odd, imaginative activities.

Into this family gathered around itself came the Klemmer kids: Inga and her slightly younger brother Rolf.

They came to ride the horses. They came to have fun. They came on weekends. They came at my father's invitation.

I was eleven then. Inga was at least fifteen—I'd seen her in the lunchroom at school—and her presence had little impact on me at the time. Rolf, on the other hand, came bringing gifts from the big city of Hudson to impress us rubes. There he is before me: squat, crew cut, his arms always half raised and his head twisting nervously on his neck every few minutes as if his collar was too tight or as if he wished to signal that he was ready for the fistfight that he knew was always imminent. And something between a sneer and smirk on his teenage face as he presents Bill with a dark-green bottle of beer. I've tagged along to the private spot he's asked to be ushered to: we're behind the barn, leaning against the stone wall, opening the bottle with his jackknife. When my turn at last comes, I gag and spit it out—warm horse piss must taste like this.

But his other gift, pulled from his inside jacket pocket, stuns me: a magazine furled up in a tight baton. Unrolled, it reveals what I could never have imagined—page after page of black and white pictures of young women in bikinis.

This mysterious artifact passed quickly into Bill's eager keeping—not without some cash exchanged.

But Bill was not destined to linger over it for long. Though he must have done his best to hide it, he lacked a realistic sense of how thoroughly Mom went through his closet and drawers as she labored to impose some order on his chaotic room. A few weeks later, I was doing one of my chores—dumping the contents of the various house wastebaskets into the little nest of flames at the bottom of the rusty oil barrel behind the garage. In went newspapers, used Kleenex, cereal boxes, clumps of my mother's hair pulled from brushes and combs—all that detritus of ordinary life that fire can reduce to sensible ash—when out of one wicker basket the magazine slid! Without a moment's hesitation, as a hero might race into a blazing building to save an infant, I plunged my arm to the elbow and yanked it out.

Now it was mine! By right of salvage. By right of my brother's despair, who—finding it gone from whatever secret spot he'd chosen—wouldn't dare to inquire any further. It was mine. But so was the peril. Perhaps my mother hadn't spoken a word to Bill—one major transgression she might pass over in silence. But if this contraband surfaced again, who knew what she might do? I stood above the smoking barrel, the magazine in my hand, tormented by indecision, when suddenly I saw I could have it both ways: I would burn the offending object—as my mother clearly wished me to—but not before tearing out several of my favorite pictures.

These rescued pages I folded into little squares no bigger than my thumb: a species of perverse origami whose creases and complications didn't create any meaningful shape, but whose unfolding revealed flowers of evil whose perfume made me dizzy. I tucked the tiny packets into the hollow of an old cherry tree nearby. Later, I moved them to the barn and hid them under a brick along one wall. Each day, after I'd fed the horses, I opened these precious packets and mooned over my beloveds.

To this day, I wonder if one of them wasn't my first sensual muse. She wore a two-piece bathing suit—it wasn't even a bikini—made out of an actual newspaper or novelty cloth printed to look that way. She smiled out at me in a way I'd never seen a woman smile. I had no idea the caption under her photo, "All the news that's fit to print," was mocking the motto of the *New York Times*, nor would I have cared. What mattered to me was that I was in thrall to her, this woman whose body was partly obscured by words, though in other places—her belly especially with its gray navel moon—language failed entirely and was replaced by the silent, astounding mystery of skin.

Alone in the hayloft, I savored these images I'd rescued from oblivion. But my joy was brief and I watched helplessly as, over the course of a few months, my precious pages moldered to a dull blur in the damp, outdoor air.

My mother's vigilance must have uncovered far more serious matters than the girlie magazine. Somehow—and here I speak not from my own memory but from the reminiscences of my mother's best friend—Mom became aware of familiarities between my father and Inga, goings-on that moved her to act with uncharacteristic vehemence. My mother's friend had just parked in front of our farmhouse one Saturday afternoon, when she heard Mom shouting:

"That girl is never to set foot in this house again! Do you hear me?"

It's possible this incident is connected to the one time I'd seen my mother cry, at the dinner table. Or perhaps memory is making things too neat, trying to tie together too many threads.

However that may be, Inga the teenaged visitor and occasional babysitter was banished from the red house, only to reappear three years later, smiling as she sauntered toward us down the marina steps that led to Dad's little sailboat.

23

Plans

I COULD SEE NOW THAT SHE WAS VERY PRETTY, SOMETHING I couldn't have noticed when I knew her before. Of course, she had changed also—now she was a young woman, slender, with a kind of distance in her thin face that, in high school when I had last seen her, had caused her classmates to call her "stuck up." Now that look had become the disdainful haughtiness of a minor princess. She no longer wore her dark hair in a ponytail, but loose over her shoulders, held back that day with a pale purple scarf that matched her dress. She would certainly have been beautiful were it not for a certain tightness in her mouth and a wariness in her eyes that gave a sense the face itself was a mask and the real person, hidden a short way behind the mask, had been hurt repeatedly and had learned some grim lessons from her treatment.

My father greeted her with a wave and big grin and offered his hand as she stepped over the little gap between the boat and the dock. With Dad at the helm giving orders, we cast off the lines and motored out and down the creek. Once we were out on the Hudson, we headed upriver under the Rip Van Winkle Bridge and finally anchored on Rodger's Island. We couldn't believe our luck—

a chance to explore a wooded island we'd seen all our lives from the bridge on various crossings and that local legend claimed had been the last refuge of the Mohican tribes.

We ran off to look around, leaving Dad showing Inga charts of the river. Half an hour later, returning to the boat, I rounded a shoreline point only a short distance from where the boat was moored to a maple trunk and saw something that confused me deeply Dad had his arms around Inga and they were kissing. Bill saw them too, and then they were aware of us and separated. We didn't say anything, and Dad hailed us with the hearty bluffness I would soon come to distrust entirely. I don't know about Bill, but I was so stunned I wanted to disbelieve what my own eyes had seen.

Such a wished-for blindness might have worked had Dad not called me on the phone a short while later to talk about "the future":

"You know, Greg, Inga has always loved you kids."

"What? I don't understand."

"She feels like you are her family. We want all of you kids to be with us."

I hung up. Who was this "we"? Who was this "us"? What new entity was my father trying to conjure out of the chaos our lives had become—this obscene pronoun made by coupling together Inga and himself? He wanted me to understand that this new unit whose destiny filled him with excitement could be expanded to include his children, if only we'd simply desert Mom as he had. For the first time in my life, a simple rage abolished all the other complicated feelings I felt for him, including the enormous longing to have him back.

Somehow, somewhere, as that summer passed into fall, Dad faltered and lost his optimistic momentum about the new life with Inga. He was never a strong man; even his most selfish and destructive impulses were short-lived and lacked conviction. Late that

September, he announced he was sorry for what he'd done, but so sorry he couldn't return to the family and must instead undertake an extravagant penance for his misbehavior. He would, he said, leave the practice he'd built up over the past eight years, leave the Hudson Valley itself, indeed leave the whole known world in order to join Medico.

Medico was a group of idealistic medical people inspired and led by Tom Dooley, a handsome young ex-Navy doctor who had set up rural clinics in the jungles of Laos. Dooley had written two books about his project, lectured widely to raise funds, and been lionized by *Life* magazine. He was a charismatic and egocentric idealist—"Like all Irish-American males, I think I'm perfect," he told a *Life* journalist.

But there were problems with Dad's adventurous new direction. He soon learned Dooley's organization only recruited bachelors— the privations involved, the low pay, the physical and medical risks—all these circumstances demanded there be no dependents. Because Dad insisted on an audience for his dramas, I knew more about his efforts to join Medico than I might have wished. I knew, for instance, that he tried to persuade the organization to take him anyway, even though he was married. To him, this was proof of his earnest desire and sincere dedication; to me, it was proof of how casually he could completely abandon us, financially and emotionally, in order to act out his fantasy. To him, a noble and desperate gesture to redeem his wrecked life; to me, a self-centered, adolescent dream of joining the French Foreign Legion. By then, Dad had seriously slipped in my opinion and I felt I could no longer count on him as a father, much as I wanted someone to guide and protect me. Still, I couldn't hate him. I saw him now as a wayward older brother—the family scamp, always getting in trouble—reckless, unreliable, and selfish, yet somehow so charming that all he did seemed, ultimately, forgivable.

Frustrated in his efforts to join Medico, he toyed with the idea of moving to Puerto Rico and setting up a practice in the hinterlands of that tropical island. Since he didn't speak a word of Spanish, the scheme was patently mad, but he took it so far that we were pulled from school and bundled onto a plane to spend a week driving the whole island in a rented car, scouting out possible locations. I remember almost nothing concrete of this trip, only a sense of bewilderment and the vague but real hope that whatever happened next would involve an attempt to put the family back together with all its original members and no intruders. The romantic cast of my father's imagination suggested this dreamed-of "new beginning" might happen in some exotic setting.

Then the answer came: an American-run hospital in a remote river valley in Haiti, the Hôpital Albert Schweitzer, needed volunteer doctors for one-year stints. The whole family could go! Even better, we wouldn't be isolated and utterly on our own as in the Puerto Rican scenario—there was an entire village of American doctors and nurses as well as a dozen families of American engineers who supervised a system of adjacent canals and irrigation ditches.

In January of 1961, a little over a year after Peter's death, we closed up our house and, in the middle of a blizzard, took the train to New York and then a series of planes to Port-au-Prince.

It's difficult to imagine what it felt like to my brothers to leave the world of Germantown. Bill lost his girlfriend and all his pals at school. Jonathan was upset at not seeing his best friend for a year. I think it hurt them badly to be yanked out of the only life they'd known. Of course, by leaving they were also escaping the shame of my father's escapades in our small town, but I think that sense of relief and escape meant more to my mother than my brothers. Nancy was only five and, for all her bright intelligence, it was hard to know how our move affected her.

My own feelings were complicated, but as with my father, my losses were almost nothing compared to what I had to gain. For him, the whole episode with Inga might simply be one of Odysseus's misadventures—not to be rectified but to be left behind. Why not simply hoist sail and set course for another island where, undoubtedly, other adventures awaited? And for me, with my secret identity as Cain, Haiti was a chance to move past the almost unbearable shame of living in a town where everyone knew I had killed my brother and caused my parents to separate out of grief over their son's death. Perhaps in Haiti I could fulfill Cain's curse and elude it also—begin my God-commanded, solitary wanderings in the wilderness, but with the possibility I'd go unrecognized there, that no one I met in this new place would guess my guilt.

24

Haiti

REMEMBERING HAITI, I FEEL LIKE SOMEONE FLOATING DOWN the Nile as it arrives at its delta: what had been a single, unified flowing becomes dispersed into a maze of rich meandering—little streams and rivulets only some of which go on to the sea. I can follow this or that wide and promising channel—note my memories and sensations—but I have no sense of where the main course of the river is, and which channels might rejoin it or which will merely dwindle to a marsh or stop short entirely at some reedy wall.

My mother saw the experience whole, at least in the first flush of arrival. I have about eight letters she wrote to her best friend back in Germantown over the nine months we were there. Mom's friend sent the letters to me a couple of years ago and they are almost the only things of my mother's I have. I read them with a mixture of greed and anguish. I want to know as much as I can about her, and I'm also hungry for any mention of myself—as if this or that casual account of my doings, deciphered correctly, will reveal at last whether or not she loved me. But I don't learn much— her tone of earnest optimism seldom lets her feelings show. On the other hand, her letters are vivid, alert, and articulate. Only a few days after our arrival, while we were still stuck in Port-au-Prince, the capital, waiting to get our Volksbus full of belongings unloaded from a freighter and passed through customs, she was already registering her impressions:

> The city itself is fascinating—it's during the height of the tourist season so all the shops are full of Americans buying liquor, Baccarat crystal, Pringle cashmere, and Wedgewood china. Greg has found that he is a born haggler and he loves it. He and Bill spent all day yesterday at the open bazaar near the pier where the boats dock. A couple of Haitian drivers even offered them a job—$1.00 for each three passengers they could talk into using their cab. The city is on a flat plain, then mountains rise very steeply just to the south up to three thousand feet. A great deal of architecture seems to be French colonial Victorian—ceilings at least fifteen feet high, louvered doors of a light mahogany, some have steeply gabled towers of the corrugated tin used on barns back home. They look almost like what I would visualize as a South Sea island's plantation owner's house. Also have heavy shutters which are usually thrown open (also usually quite in need of repair). All these are in the city—all these are older buildings, and then sandwiched in between will be ramshackle hovels (two rooms). The family home in the back and in the front one glass cabinet with a few groceries and then shelves lined with Babincourt rum, boxes of Fab and the oddest miscellany possible! Houses out in the country are made of poles, then covered with stucco and a thatched roof. I haven't seen the worst of the slums yet but Jim says they're worse than San Juan.
>
> Smells and noises impress me the most. Most of the cooking is done outdoors over wood or charcoal fire in a brazier—everything is fried so there is a constant and distinctive odor of frying too and at the same time of burning rubbish.

She's right—I loved to haggle in the markets. It was the first of many pleasures I found in Haiti. There wasn't a single fixed price in the entire world of the open air market, except for the fifty centime you paid for the little yellow, green, or blue two-packs of Chicklets gum spread out in a woman's flat basket at each street corner. Everything else cost somewhere between the ludicrously high price the merchant first named and the equally absurd counteroffer with which you responded. Between these two figures was the realm of negotiation and street theater—wisecracks and grimaces, exaggerated gestures of incredulity and feigned contempt, comical asides to the invariable onlookers. I picked up Creole as quickly as I could in order to be part of this chaotic world of pantomime and verbal game that gave as much delight as any actual purchase or sale. Shy as I was, I took great delight in entertaining the market crowd with the sight of a pint-sized, wide-eyed *"ti blanc"* exclaiming *"Mon dieu, mwe pas fou!"* ("My God, I'm not crazy!") to a vendor's initial proposal. But even to stroll among the dense confusion of proffered objects filled me with pleasure: the bolts of bright cloth, straw hats, and carvings of Port-au-Prince or the more down-to-earth offerings in rural markets—machetes and cotton shirts, gnarled manioc roots, green-skinned oranges, beans and rice, and spices and herbs in dark, powdery heaps.

At first, the smells of Haiti were overwhelming: the rot of mangoes, urine and feces and ripe fruit, frying plantain, spices and sweat, and the whole mixture baked in tropical heat and permeated completely by the pungent, sweet smoke of charcoal. What was intense to the point of nausea those first weeks, became, in time, a smell I loved so completely I still hunger for it. To this day, the whiff of a suburban brazier or garbage left out in summer heat can transport me, make me briefly dizzy with the hope I am in Haiti again.

When the last of a long series of bribes had finally cleared our car and possessions from customs, we started up the coast road, pausing in each town outside the ocher Army post while grim-faced soldiers with ancient bolt-action rifles looked over our papers and peered in through the windows. It was a three-hour drive along the coast and then inland up the main river valley of the Artibonite over a bumpy and sometimes washed-out dirt road, but at last we arrived at the hamlet of Deschapelles.

The Hôpital Albert Schweitzer was a recently built, sprawling one-story structure made from local stone. It had been built by Larimer Mellon and his wife, Gwen. He'd been born into one of the richest of American families and lived a life of ease until, on an African safari, he encountered Dr. Schweitzer at his jungle hospital. Mellon was so moved by Schweitzer's presence and sense of mission that, in his mid-forties, he enrolled in medical school. His wife, a Philadelphia heiress, responded by going to nursing school. Their studies completed, they considered where to go next. Haiti was— and still is—easily the most disease-ridden and impoverished country in the Western hemisphere, and so it seemed a good place to start their life of service. The Mellons built the hospital and a house nearby and then settled permanently into their healing project. The hospital's half-dozen staff doctors worked for minimal salaries, rotating in and out on year-long shifts from the States. There was also a group of Mennonite nurses and public works people and a small contingent of Catholic nun volunteers. When we arrived, the Mellons were in their mid-fifties and worked, like everyone else, daily twelve-hour shifts at the hospital.

The hospital had an operating room, which was difficult to keep sterile, surrounded as it was by rampant tropical infection, and it had its own generators for electricity, a cafeteria for staff and workers, and a few rooms with beds for the very ill. But mostly it was designed for outpatient clinics. The diseased would come or be brought from twenty or more miles away by *camion* or foot or burro. Those who brought them would tether their burros in the open, stone-floored courtyard abutting the main hospital wall and set up camp on the lawn. Crossing the main lawn to the hospital veranda meant threading my way through forty or more families gathered around their small charcoal cooking fires. As I passed, a squatting woman might look up, her hair bound back tight in a faded head scarf worn pirate-style, her face carved by hunger to the dark mahogany dignity of a skull that has the will to live, or a child of two might stare at me, wide-eyed and impassive.

To leave behind the flat outdoor light, acid in its intensity, and the heat that pressed down like an iron, to pass through the screen doors into the sudden dark of the hospital itself, was to stand awhile blinking. The long corridors that led away in three directions from the lobby were dark with huddled bodies, standing or sitting or prone. Here, the reek of misery and disease, unrelieved by any breeze or other tropic smell, was enough to make me dizzy. These were the clinic patients, waiting hour after hour for the chance to see the doctor briefly or perhaps only his Haitian assistant and then, no matter how sick, then returning to the lawn where they'd sleep in the open on a straw mat.

The suffering from disease and malnutrition in Haiti was almost inconceivable. Three-quarters of the children in any village had the shrunken bodies and swollen bellies of advanced malnutrition—and those were the children who had lived. Three out of five died before they reached the age of six. Everyone had parasites—hookworm and tapeworm especially. Malaria, tuberculosis, dysentery, dengue fever, and a host of other awful ailments were also rampant. Though its goal was to be modern and reasonably clean, the Hôpital Albert Schweitzer was overwhelmed by disease as surely as the ruins of the valley's colonial sugar mills were engulfed by vines; driving along the canal road you might see the broken remnant of a white stone arch like the hand of a drowning man thrust above green water, but the jungle had won.

The country should have been a paradise; back in the eighteenth century it had been prosperous and fertile and had been known as "the Pearl of the Antilles." The first Spanish settlers had exterminated the native inhabitants, and later the French had repopulated the island with African slaves brought to work the sugar plantations. These same slaves bravely revolted and defeated several of Napoleon's armies and by 1807 the French were gone. From then on, the land was governed by one dictator after another. Ironically, that early freedom from the colonial system set forces in motion that destroyed the environment. The slash-and-burn pattern of farming that made sense on the huge continent of mainland Africa— a field cleared of jungle, planted, then abandoned when the thin soil gave out—was a bad idea on an island like Haiti where flat land—a few river valleys and a narrow coastal plain—was limited and where the rest of the land was an endless wrinkle of steep-sided mountains.

All cooking was done with charcoal, which takes a lot of wood to make. Over the course of two centuries the mountains were shaved bare of forests and what soil was left steadily eroded. Only the daily deluge of the rainy season kept anything growing at all, but even that contributed to erosion. A large, American-built dam and irrigation ditches made the Artibonite Valley the richest and most stable agricultural area in the country, but even in our region count- less people were starving to death.

Haiti's politics were as grim as its economics. While we were there, in 1961, Castro's Cuba—only thirty or so miles from the north coast—was exporting little invasion groups to the neighboring Dominican Republic and threatening the same to other Caribbean islands. Boats would drop small groups of commandos at remote spots on the Dominican coast; they'd move inland, set up camps, and dream of revolution. There was much talk that Haiti was vul- nerable to such infiltrations, but anyone who lived in Haiti had a good laugh about that. Why would Castro want Haiti? Why would any government whose political credibility rested on improving the lot of its people take on the vast and insoluble problems of Haiti? Everyone knew the U.S. government paid money to "Papa Doc" Duvalier, the current dictator in Port-au-Prince, to simply stay quiet and keep the world ignorant of his country's existence and the appalling extent of its miseries. Papa Doc himself was a lesson in despair and corruption—he'd begun as an idealistic, American-trained doctor fighting smallpox in the hills. Now he was just one more in an endless succession of greedy and brutal rulers, hiding in his white palace while his face, owlish and bespectacled, glowered out from the gray ovals on the corner of each colorful Haitian postage stamp.

Democracy Haitian-style was shameless. Shortly after we arrived, an election was held for the National Assembly—a ridiculous sham since only candidates from Duvalier's party could run. Still, it was not without its surprise—each and every official ballot had "Long Live Papa Doc!" printed in bold letters at the bottom. After the election, government radio jubilantly announced the discovery of this phrase on the ballots and could only conclude that each and every voter had scrawled his spontaneous wish that Papa Doc become "President-for-Life." Duvalier had no choice, the radio voice continued, but to yield to the will of the people.

Against all the almost unimaginable suffering, oppression, and environmental deterioration, you had to set this: the mysterious and undeniable fact of the Haitian people's joy and gentleness. It was real, not the product of some tourist bureau's imagination. It was simply there—inexplicable, but palpable. You heard it in the voices and gestures, in the expressions of dignity on faces. Everyone I've ever known who has lived in Haiti has felt it. No one I know has ever been able to explain it.

25

My Mother's Letters

WHEN I READ MY MOTHER'S LETTERS TO HER FRIEND BACK in Germantown, I'm struck by their restraint. Even writing to her best friend, she didn't let down her guard of cheerful alertness. Her letters focus resolutely on the world around her.

She's gamely, though erratically, trying to school all of us kids. The correspondence courses she arranged before we left seem to have fallen through, and she writes things like: "Bill, Greg, and I are doing the middle of elementary algebra and will go on from there. Since Jon is studying the Middle Ages, we've spent an hour each morning this week reading from a paperback of mine on *Medieval People*—Bill, Greg, and I have enjoyed it immensely—some of it a little above Jon but not too much. Also read *MacBeth* aloud last week and next week will go back to it again. My main problem is discipline—all three boys start giggling and fooling and it's sometimes *very* difficult." After a few months, this effort at home schooling will dwindle to nothing and my ninth grade slate will be blissfully blank of algebra.

"Greg's still reading omnivorously." How I grab hold of these terse sentences. Her relationship with us was as matter-of-fact as her phrases about us, and as I reread them I have a hopeless feeling as I try to discover an interior dimension. My mother's attention had no obvious emotional component. She could be impressed or even approving, but her approval never reached a level of intensity that demanded expression in hugs or kisses or any other form of physical contact. Even a direct word of approval was rare.

Ever since the hunting accident, I had hoped to communicate to her my agony over Peter's death. I knew she was a fundamentally reserved person, but I needed to believe she'd listen and respond. Shortly after our arrival in Haiti, I thought I saw my opportunity. The family seemed to have stabilized sufficiently—we were all living under the same roof again, the simple routines of our life were reestablished. It was February 3—my birthday—surely this was an auspicious moment to risk seeking the acknowledgment and forgiveness I desperately needed.

We were having a family dinner, all of us seated at the dark, elongated table that was set in the central room to catch whatever crossbreezes the open windows on either side might create. Even Dad was there, the hospital's proximity allowing him a half-hour dinner between afternoon and evening clinics. When my cake was brought in with its fourteen candles, I got up and ran into the room I shared with my brothers, threw myself down on my bed and sobbed. After awhile, Mom entered and sat down on the mattress beside me. I kept crying, my face pressed down into the red-ribbed cotton coverlet.

"What's the matter?" she asked.

"It's Peter," I said, looking up at where she sat with her hands in her lap. The sad, serious set of her face didn't change at his name— I'm sure she already knew. I hid my face again and my crying was tearless now, a series of small moans that was all I could manage though I had been desperate before to speak urgent, clear words to her. It was as if all my misery had clotted in my throat with the taboo syllables of my brother's name. She sat there next to me for a while, near me but not touching me or saying a word, and then finally she stood up and left the room, closing the door quietly behind her.

26

The Paths

SO MANY GOOD THINGS SEEMED TO HAVE COME OF THE MOVE to Haiti. We had reconstituted our family as a physical unit and consolidated our lives into the ten acres of the Deschapelles compound. Dad was busy with interesting if exhausting work at the hospital. For the first time in his life, his medical training was saving lives and relieving deep suffering on a daily basis. Mom seemed in better spirits than she had been in over a year. We kids wanted nothing more than to believe that this improbable family healing was real, and that the nightmare that had preceded it was over for good. But after the experience on my birthday, I felt I wasn't really a part of the family anymore. My mother's response confirmed what I had suspected: Peter's death had put an uncrossable wall between myself and the rest of them. I felt certain nothing I could ever do would redeem me in their eyes.

These grim thoughts hurt me deeply, but there was also something irrepressible about me. If I couldn't find warmth and forgiveness inside my family, I would turn outward and explore my new surroundings.

Haiti is a vast network of paths. True, the brightly painted and fancifully named pickup trucks called *camiones* zipped from village to village on rutted dirt roads, loaded down with sacks and straw bags, tethered pigs, crates of chickens and passengers crowding the rows of wooden benches set up in the truck bed, but the real story of how everyone moved around was barefoot on paths. Paths went everywhere, crisscrossing and intersecting with the bewildering intensity of capillaries in a human body.

The hamlet of Deschapelles was located on low hills on the southern side of the Artibonite Valley, which was about eight miles wide at that point. The valley floor was flat and the American engineers had built and maintained an elaborate series of irrigation canals that allowed rice to be grown throughout the bottomlands. Many of the paths in the valley proper followed the geometry of palm-lined rice paddy borders, but up behind the hospital the hills rose toward a tumult of mountains, and that direction beckoned.

The hills were dry and deforested, but even the steepest slopes had been conjured into garden plots worked by hand with hoes. The soil was chalky and thin and the fields studded with pocked volcanic rock crisscrossed by thick gray lizards. Up there, most crops withered when the rainy season was gone, though the fence of stringy cactus around a whitewashed hut might grow so dense not even the skinny black pigs that rooted everywhere could squeeze through. Most of the heat-stunned uplands were either dry fields with only the occasional breadfruit tree left standing, or else thickets of thorny scrub, but the gullies and gorges that marked streambeds or seasonal runoffs were still dense with trees.

I liked nothing more than packing sandwiches and a canteen and heading out on my own for four or five hours at a time, wandering aimlessly along the endless paths, letting myself get lost. I had the excitement of constantly being in unknown territory without any real anxiety, because I knew all the paths connected up and I would eventually work my way back toward some recognizable place or vista. On those journeys I was so alone and so alive I was no longer Cain at all, and could almost imagine myself Adam roaming a bedraggled Eden. I was free of my history and almost all I saw was new, brought close to the dazzle and strangeness, the sensual intensity of earth in its first days.

Whenever I descended a path into a deeply wooded gully, I began to feel a vague excitement, a sense of mystery that drew me on. This gully might channel a shallow stream, and if so, I might come upon women and girls doing their washing. Crouched there in little groups, bare-breasted in the sun-dappled shallows, they chattered away as they soaked each garment, bunched it up and pounded it against a rock, then spread it smooth on a boulder to dry. If I saw such a gathering, I hung back in the shadows watching as long as I could, until I was at last spotted, at which point I had no choice but to continue my walk, now crimson-red and with averted eyes, their teasing cries following me as I crossed the stream and made my way up the other side.

Once I was walking down a narrow path that had been worn hip-deep into the limestone hill itself by centuries of bare feet, when I suddenly found myself face to face with a beautiful young woman returning from the spring with a huge calabash gourd full of water balanced on her head. In her dress faded to colorlessness, she could have been a princess under a spell—her crown transformed into this green gourd which she still wore with royal dignity. She stopped and stood as much to the side as she could and closed her heavy-lidded eyes as if that made her invisible. To pass by, I had to brush so close I could smell her skin.

27

Voodun

IN THE TWENTY HOUSES AND BUNGALOWS THAT MADE UP the American compound in Deschapelles, there was a persistent, subdued tension between the engineers and the hospital personnel. The hospital people lived in about twenty stone houses and two long wooden bungalows, one for the Catholic nuns, another for the Mennonites. The American engineers lived in seven newer cement-block houses, each hidden behind a tall hibiscus hedge. Their Haitian counterparts in the irrigation project, another five or six families, kept to themselves in another set of new houses. To us, the American engineers and their families seemed a pretty rough bunch —they drank a fair bit at their clubhouse and walking past their houses at night you might well hear shouting and swearing.

On the hospital side, there were the doctors and medical personnel and a Methodist minister. Though I don't think there was any religious requirement for the hospital crowd, the Mellons were very pious in a quiet way and they set the tone for our part of the camp. Each Saturday evening, the minister and his wife arranged rows of wooden benches on a run-down tennis court behind the community building so that, for several hours, local worshipers could sing hymns in Creole while insects and moths swirled above them in the white cone of a floodlight beam. That same evening, the engineers punctuated the week with an American movie in their clubhouse. The movies were invariably ancient black-and-white Westerns of the Hopalong Cassidy era, but all the American kids in the camp attended, as did scores of local Haitians. Packed solid in that unventilated space, clutching cold bottles of the local Couronne soda and cheering on the heroes, we were a raucous, redolent crowd.

To take the short way home after the movies, we skirted the clubhouse pool that glowed like a giant blue coffin, then cut through the minister's backyard, where the perfume of the night-blooming jasmine bush was dense as a butterfly cloud, then out onto a path that edged the tennis court and led to our own house on the outskirts. Sometimes the congregants, in their bright dresses and pressed shirts, would still be singing as my brothers and I went past.

Around them, around us all, was the huge dark of voodun or voodoo. Once you were beyond the tennis courts, you could hear its heart beating in the drums. Voodun was the abiding, indigenous mystery—the religion Haitians had amalgamated out of the rites and rituals brought on the slave ships from West Africa. Christianity was only a pale veneer over the dark wood of voodun. There was a saying that Haiti is 70 percent Catholic, 30 percent Protestant, and 100 percent Voodun. No Haitian, asked directly by a foreigner, had much to say about voodun, but it was always there, especially in the hinterlands where we lived—omnipresent and invisible. It was most powerfully present at night and then mundanely so in the daylight —like the huge mapou tree at the crossroads just below the hospital whose root niches and crannies would be stuck with candles burned down to stubs, gifts for the spirits who lived inside it. At night, with its wrinkled, elephant-skin bark alive with small flames, the mapou must have been an eerie sight. In daylight all that mystery dispersed

and it had the bleak feel of a yard at dawn after a party—the pud-
dled candles like crushed paper cups revelers had left.

Nights, over the hubbub of village sounds, you could always
hear the drums somewhere, either far away or not that far, and know
that a ceremony was taking place. But it was impossible to find that
place. More than once I'd gone out at night to search. I moved only
along the main paths I knew, through the clusters of huts below the
hospital, trying to gauge the direction of the sound. I never seemed
to be far from its source, but I could also never get any closer and
finally the erratic tempo of my own edgy heart would win out over
the drums and I'd turn back toward the safety of camp.

28

Last Letter

MANY OF MY MOTHER'S LETTERS TO HER BEST FRIEND IN Germantown were haunted by the question of whether or not our family would return there when the year's work in Haiti was up. It's clear from what she writes that many of my father's patients felt deserted when he left town so suddenly. Another doctor had set up a practice in Germantown by then and he seemed, in my parents' eyes, to be exploiting this rift and—was this part of the problem also?—raising as many moral questions as possible about my father. Whatever the reason, Mom's letters to her friend were not just personal—they were also designed to send messages to the larger community.

At a certain point the Germantown Board of Supervisors was considering advertising for a new doctor and so, in August, she wrote:

> We feel definitely committed to going back and are looking forward to it. We're certain that all our personal problems are finally and irrevocably resolved and want to get back to work there. But if a third man is coming in it would be foolish. Jim would plan to convert his mother's garage to a waiting room but it will require heat, extra window, etc., and would mean starting in with letters and plans in the near future. We

can't commit ourselves to that investment without more certainty. . . . I wonder if Brownie's death with Jim so far away had antagonized people against him—that he wasn't there and should have been. . . . We are both aware that many people would never come back to Jim as patients and can understand their annoyance at his leaving. Do you honestly think there are enough of them who still want him to return? If that's not the case don't try to soften any statement or blunt the edge of it— the more definite the better. After all, we've taken a great deal this past two years and can take more. We can move somewhere else and start again, and I'm certain we'd make out very well, but we have many friends in Germantown and would prefer to be there.

When she wrote this, her last letter, she must have known her marriage was over. Dad's mother, Brownie, had died in early July and he'd returned for the funeral. But when the funeral was over, he stayed on stateside for another full week. I learned more about that incident many years later from my father's sister, Aunt Doe.

"Well, your father was always a spoiled kid who thought he could get away with anything. Mom and Dad spoiled him right from the beginning. I never liked him, but I did my best to keep it to myself until he pulled that stunt at Brownie's funeral."

"What do you mean?"

"Well, frankly, Greg, it was because of that I haven't spoken to your father for forty years. His behavior was scandalous. When Brownie died, your father came back from Haiti and your uncle and I drove down seven hours from New Hampshire for the funeral. Well, Greg, that night, when we were supposed to sit with Brownie's casket, your father was out gallivanting with his girlfriend. Your uncle and I sat alone in the funeral parlor greeting Brownie's friends. We didn't know anybody in that town. It was so embarrassing. I couldn't believe even your father could be so irresponsible and callous. When I finally saw him the next day at the funeral I said to him, 'Jim, this is it. I don't want to ever speak to you again.'

Can you imagine what those friends of your grandmother's thought, or the whole town for that matter?"

I'll never know if my mother knew the details of this escapade, but when, after the funeral, my father lingered on stateside for another whole week my mother knew what that meant, no matter what explanations my father gave.

I must have entered the living room just after Mom read the telegram from Dad saying his return would be delayed. She was sitting on the couch, sobbing quietly.

"Mom, what's wrong?" I asked.

"Nothing," she said. "I just miss your father and he can't get back for another week."

It was a very complicated moment for me—the instant I saw her crying I felt the whole facade of our year in Haiti crumble. I saw my mother vulnerable, saw her yield to sad feelings, and this gave me a half-conscious sense of hope for my own situation. She had rejected my birthday plea for forgiveness, but that had been a plea out of my anguish toward her defended strength. Now that she, too, had been overwhelmed, perhaps we could once again, at some future date, enter into a negotiation that might make both our sufferings bearable. I loved her so much. Even as I watched her struggle to regain control and brush aside my questions about what was wrong, I clung to an image of the two of us weeping in each other's arms. I didn't want or hope for happiness, only some release, some sluicing away of all the accumulated grief.

29

The Operation

ONLY A WEEK OR SO AFTER MY FATHER RETURNED FROM Brownie's funeral, my mother entered the Deschapelles hospital for what we were told was a minor surgical procedure that would only keep her overnight. I know now it was a D & C, a procedure that involves scraping the lining of the uterus.

Maybe no operation in the tropics is ever really minor, especially in the conditions prevailing at Hôpital Albert Schweitzer. About a year after we came back from Haiti, my mother's best friend was riding her horse down the street in Germantown when my father came out of his office to admire it. "That's a beautiful gelding," he said. "In Haiti, we didn't have any—they were either mares or stallions. You couldn't risk an operation there because of infections." The woman's immediate, unspoken thought was "My God, Jim, what are you saying? What about Barbara?" My father patted the horse and then went back inside.

The mysteries surrounding that operation have never been addressed. I'll never know why my mother didn't fly to Miami for the surgery, or at the very least go to the main hospital in Port-au-Prince. Or if the operation was truly elective, as a D & C usually is, why she didn't wait four months until we returned to the States. I understand my mother well enough to know she would have felt what was good enough for Haitian patients was good enough for her. Her stubborn high-mindedness was something we all admired. But she couldn't have chosen to have the operation in Deschapelles without my father's consent and assistance. He knew childhood rheumatic fever had left her with a scarred, weakened heart. And he knew how easily infections happened in the tropics. How much did he care about her at this point? How much did he want her to live? The decision to have the surgery in Deschapelles put her life in the balance; her fate was precarious—impossible to know which way it would go. Sometimes I see what happened as one more bit of recklessness; sometimes I'm haunted by the image of my father surreptitiously placing a finger on one side of the scales, tipping it just slightly.

She went in early one morning. Jon and I were invited to visit her that same afternoon, while Bill was out laying water pipe with the community development people and Nancy stayed with neighbors. We had lunch with Dad in the hospital cafeteria, then someone took us to her while Dad returned to his endless line of patients at clinic. As soon as we entered her room, we knew something was seriously wrong. Her face was contracted in pain and she gasped for each breath. Jon and I stood there, unable to move, as we watched her struggle interrupted by harsh coughs and long, agonizing shudders that racked her whole body. She kept trying to speak, but couldn't. She was too weak to sit up and only after great effort propped herself on one elbow. She gestured in a way meant to be reassuring but that instead seemed like the imploring, spasmodic motions of someone drowning. I left the room and ran toward the examining room where Dad was.

"Dad, you've got to come quick! It's Mom. She can't breathe."

We raced back to the room, stopping to get Dr. Swenk, the surgeon, on the way. Mom collapsed back down onto the mattress as they entered.

"Go home, kids," my father said. "Your mother will be OK. You can help by staying out of the way and behaving yourselves," and he pushed us out into the dark hall crowded with clinic patients.

I never saw her again. Dad wasn't home for dinner, but he sent word she was doing fine. In the middle of the night, I heard Dad enter our bedroom and sit down on the foot of Bill's bed. He began to sob and repeat aloud again and again in a hopeless voice: "What will we do now? What will we do?"

30

Leaving

TWO DAYS LATER, MY MOTHER WAS BURIED. THEY HELD THE funeral in the bungalow that served as a church, just down the street from our house. Her children were not invited.

I have in my memory a single, obsessive image: the scene of our not grieving suspended in time—waiting to be freed. Bill and Jon and I are sitting on our beds in the Deschapelles house and we hear a bell ringing. I hear that bell now, its imagined movement the only motion—a slow tolling and then it stops like a stilled heart. That bell marked the beginning or the end of my mother's memorial service—the three of us looked at each other, but no one said a word. These three brothers can't leave that scene. All that moment's misery and sorrow is locked up inside them, closed off—they've become statues, a stone tableau. Time flows over them like a watery breeze, but they can't move or change. They don't deserve to be left in that room bereft of the tears that might help them, might melt them back into the river of time.

Now Dad was in charge entirely, the only adult guiding and guarding us. Grieving would take its cues from him. Which is to say, there would be no grieving, but instead fortitude and action and a sudden departure like flight from the scene of a crime. Fleeing was the pattern in all our intimate losses—hadn't Aunt Doe, sixty years later, still been uneasy about how quickly they had left the day of Charley Hayes's death; and hadn't we moved from the Alcove farm to Renssalaerville just after Christopher's death? When Peter died, Dad fled, and now, now . . . wasn't this the greatest of our losses? To lose your mother, to lose your loved mother when you are still a child— when that happens you need to lie down on the earth and mix your tears with the dust, you need to pour ashes on your head and wail, not pack a suitcase and depart without ever even seeing her grave.

Dad must have brushed aside all offers of consolation—I don't remember seeing anyone in our house then. Within days of her death, we were leaving, on our way back to the States.

I was in shock. Almost everything from that time is a blank except one episode from the journey back. We were all standing in front of an airline desk in Miami when the woman behind the counter noticed my sister, Nancy, who'd just turned six. With her long blond curls bleached white by the sun and her deep tan, she was a striking sight.

"My what a lovely little girl," the woman said. "Your mother must be very proud of you."

"Her mother's dead," my father responded in his best matter-of-fact voice.

The woman stammered, "I'm so sorry. How awful."

"That's OK," he replied calmly. "She'll have to get used to it."

31

The Green Bird

ONCE, WANDERING ALONG PATHS IN THE DUSTY, SCRUB-BRUSH
foothills behind the hospital in Haiti, I saw a tiny bird, far smaller
than a sparrow, flit past me and vanish. It was a pale, bright green—
the color of just-opened leaves on a lilac bush before the sunlight
darkens and lacquers them. The bird went by so fast I couldn't see
much of it, couldn't find it again though I tried to follow where it
had disappeared into some taller trees.

Later, when I described the bird, no one knew its name or even
recalled ever having seen one. Without a name for it, I had nothing
to mediate between me and my amazement; no way to assign the
tiny bird a neat, labeled place in my experience. Instead, it flits,
nameless and vivid still, through my memory. Sometimes, because
it hurts me to see the small creature vanish among the trees without
a trace, I call it "Ti Oiseau," which is the title of a Haitian song and
means "little bird" in Creole. Versions of that song have made it out
of Haiti into our jukeboxes, borne north by one of those warm currents that periodically carry the tropical rhythms of calypso or other
Caribbean sounds toward our colder culture.

"Ti Oiseau," especially the export version, has upbeat rhythmic elements, but ultimately it's a plaintive, melancholy song about lost love and makes me think now of "Greensleeves," which was my mother's favorite song.

When I hum "Ti Oiseau," sights and sounds and smells from Haiti come back to me with the bittersweet of nostalgia and all that is lost. But when I hum "Greensleeves," I feel an imageless, infinite sadness that fills my body and presses out against my ribs as if there isn't enough room in me for both this feeling and the air I need to live.

Part Four

32

Back to Germantown

AND SO BEGAN THE NEW REGIME. DAD, WITH NOT A nurturing bone in his body, herded us home. The Orr brood, minus Mom, minus another member, staggered back north. North, where we were known, but where everything before us was unknown.

Dad threw himself back into the work of rebuilding a practice he'd left in ruins. The rest of us were essentially abandoned, but no one in town dared meddle or inquire too much into how we were surviving. School began again shortly after our return and that was a blessing with its bustle and structure. But when school was over and we took the long bus ride home to our place fifteen miles east of town, we were returning to a deep desolation. The old house seemed darker than ever after the saturating light of Haiti. It was as though there were fewer lamps, or no matter how many lamps you turned on, there still wasn't enough light to push back the dark. It was as though the steady, subdued glow of my mother—like a statue of the Virgin Mary, folded in on its sorrow but still shedding light—was gone now and the gloom ruled entire.

We seldom saw Dad. For a while, he hired a woman to come in the afternoon and leave a meal in pots on the stove, but she had kids and a husband of her own and left as soon as we got off the bus in late afternoon. She wasn't unfriendly, but there was always a sense that we had only borrowed or rented her—that she belonged to some other family and this was only a job. Once she left, we were on our own until bedtime. Most nights we never saw Dad at all, though twice a week and on weekends he had evening hours in the office rooms in the back of the house and on those nights he'd duck in for a moment around dinner to "check" on us. We'd be in bed before he'd seen his last patients and he'd either be gone before we woke or sleeping in past our leaving on the bus.

We basically fended for ourselves in a haphazard, improvised way. Bill, sixteen years old now, made an effort to cook a hot meal for us on weekend evenings, but the rest was scavenge as scavenge can. Each of us developed a certain, intense loyalty to a simple dinner we could make on our own: hot dogs, peanut butter and jelly sandwiches, cold cereal.

Orr humor had always favored irony, that mode in which the head mocks the heart and bares its intellectual teeth at what it sees as a hostile world. Now Dad introduced us to a joke so dark and apropos it quickly became the official family joke and, for years afterward, its final lines would be invoked by one or another of us when some sudden disaster struck. "Four guys," it began, "were going camping. None of them wanted to cook, so they decided to alternate the chore until one of them complained about the quality of the food. They all agreed that whoever complained first would be stuck with the cooking job for the rest of the trip. The first night's designated cook decided, 'the hell with this,' and mixed three or four balls of ripe horse manure into his stew, served it up on tin plates and sat back to watch his buddies eat. The first guy to swallow a mouthful, spat it out and screamed, 'Horse manure!' Then, missing only a single beat, he added, 'But good, but good.'"

We found this joke hilarious. It was a perverse hymn of praise to our family's powers of digestion. We could take anything no matter how awful; we could adapt and survive. I laughed to tears and stomach cramps at these hapless, pathetic males on their own with no one to care for them and caring for no one. I didn't realize then it was my father's joke, a joke on us, a joke in which it's every man for himself. A joke in which the guy by the campfire who spits out the poisoned stew may seem a fool, but he's also crafty Odysseus who thinks fast as lightning and outwits anyone who tries to hem him in.

33

Inga

NOT ALL DAD'S WEEKENDS THAT FALL OF OUR RETURN WERE
spent on house calls, nor all his evenings at office hours. Without
our knowing it, he had resumed his romance with Inga. As the
months went by, he would gradually let slip her name—testing the
waters. Four or five months after we returned, we finally saw her
again. They'd been out the night before and late one Sunday morning, she and Dad arrived at the house with a bag of groceries and
the announcement that she would cook us a meal. We were all awkwardly introduced as if somehow we were meeting for the first time.

She must have been all of twenty by then. During the year we'd
been in Haiti, she'd been a lady's companion for an elderly woman
in New York. Her features were sharper, more alert. One moment
you could look at the sculpted planes of her face and say she was
beautiful, but a second later she was a bird of prey. My father didn't
know it then, but she was more than a match for him. Dad concealed
his narcissism under a polished veneer of charm, but she had no
such need to fool herself or others—her version was wild, violent,
and uninhibited. Soon enough, he would learn—the knife scar she
created along his ribs would itself be the rueful smile of his new

knowledge. Soon enough, there would be suicide attempts, some serious, some not; soon enough, she'd gather as many of our old family photos as she could and burn them in the fireplace; soon enough, in vivid, homicidal rages she'd chase Bill or me through the house with a frying pan, or, more ludicrously, with a kettle of hot tea water from the stove.

But all that was in the future, waiting to unfold. For now, there was simply the awkwardness of entering a household from which, not long before, she had been banned; of meeting Bill and me again, both of whom knew of her earlier affair with Dad. She must have felt deep in enemy territory. That her rival was dead was a fact, but from the way she moved nervously through the house, it was clear she felt Mom might have left it booby-trapped.

The dinner demonstration went off as planned and soon we saw far more of her. By early spring, the inevitable was announced—she and Dad were to be married. A date was set. In the intervening time, Dad made a point of being alone with each of us kids at least once to talk about their relationship and the upcoming marriage. Among other things, he seemed to need us to give our approval. I was very uncomfortable, but what he did really wasn't my business and he was convinced the marriage was essential to his happiness and would help to make the wreckage of our living arrangements into something more homelike.

Having secured everyone's approval, Dad moved on to a further request: we must all go to the wedding. Our presence there was essential, a public proof we endorsed the event. I balked. I couldn't agree to go. Bill and Jon and Nancy had given in, and Dad had them try to persuade me "for the sake of family peace."

The morning of the wedding, Dad was dressed in his tuxedo. My brothers and sister were spiffed up and already waiting in the car outside as Dad tried one last time to convince me. I was in my room. He yelled a summons from the waiting room near his back office. I started down the stairs toward him and paused halfway down. The steps were painted a robin's-egg blue and as Dad began talking in his most serious, solemn tone, I felt dizzy and sat down to steady myself. He climbed up the lower steps so that he loomed over me.

"Look, I'm asking you one last time to go. I need you to do this for me."

"I'm sorry," I said. "I told you, I can't."

"Why not?" he demanded.

"I just can't."

"Listen, this is the only time I'm ever going to beg you to do something for me. You must."

"I can't."

"What do you mean, you can't?"

"Because of Mom. "

Now, Dad shifted from pleading to threats. He was angry.

"Listen to me, sport, you're making a big mistake. If you don't get in the car right this minute, I'll never forgive you."

Now I was weeping and telling him how sorry I was. I squeezed my hands between my legs and rested my head on my knees, sobbing, unable to look up. He yelled at me a little while longer. Finally, he gave up and walked out, slamming the door behind him.

I sat for a while, feeling the emptiness of the house, watching the blank, lemony glare of morning light slant through the windows onto the empty chairs and the low table cluttered with magazines. Then I climbed the stairs and went back into my room. Closing the door made me feel safer. Not safe, but safer.

34

School

IN THE BEGINNING, I BELIEVED IN SCHOOL THE WAY PIOUS and naive monks probably believed in the medieval church. The reality of school might be blurry or harsh or confusing, but the idea was lucid and just: a white city on a high hill whose walls were made entirely of mimeographed quizzes—it shone from within with a splendid glow and the little red-circled grades the teacher made with her pen were like rosette windows through which the pure glory of God's judgment light streamed.

For the most part, my actual early experiences confirmed my sense of belonging to a coherent and humane institution. Of course, there was the periodic teacher like Mrs. Henderson in third grade, who seemed to have stepped out of the Spanish Inquisition: she gave me D's in "Eats Well" and "Plays Well with Others" and stationed herself next to the line of garbage cans in the lunchroom where she inspected everyone's tray. She invariably found the coleslaw I'd stuffed into my empty milk carton and sent me back to my seat to fish it out and finish it. But then I console myself by lingering over memories of Miss Buswell rewarding our fifth-grade class for straightening our desks at the end of each day by reading aloud from *The Otter Family* and all of us, even the hardest cases, even Eddie Whitney who'd eat white paste on a dare, weeping quietly when the mother otter got her paw caught in the steel jaw of a trap. Then I believe again, I am brought back into the fold of Mother School and think: "Yes, there is a bosom here, capacious as Miss Buswell's, on which all the sad young things can sob and be restored; there is a capacity to reward the forlorn ones who come seeking love and approval."

The intensity of my faith itself had a fatal feel. My deep need for order hinted at equally deep doubts hidden within. Even before Peter's death, I'd begun to lose my status as a certified teacher's pet—something stubborn or suspicious emerged in me and I began to drift farther back in the classroom, farther away from the front row desks where alertness reigned.

And then, there was the trauma of Peter's death and its aftermath. When Peter died and I heard of the uncanny coincidence of Charley Hayes's death, I thought I was staring into the destructive face of God—a face like a dark mirror in which I saw my own face reflected back to me as Cain. Cain's story could carry me forward, where my own human identity, that of a twelve-year-old boy, could not. That grim identification sustained me through my parents' separation and even through my mother's sudden death. Both these catastrophes seemed the indirect but clear result of Peter's death. But my father's marriage to Inga felt different. Her violent instability seemed a thing of its own, a vengeful entity unrelated to Cain. I felt my identification with Cain beginning to lose its explanatory power.

Violent trauma shreds the web of meaning. It destroys all the threads of relationship that link the hurt self to the world—to other people and objects, or to nature, or even to the inner world of its own feelings. The real task of a trauma victim—the task that makes life worth living again—is to reconnect the self to the world. To do that, you need to reweave the web, to risk the spinning of new threads until they form a sustaining pattern the self can inhabit.

I didn't do this. On the day of Peter's death, I heard every thread in my web snap in a single instant. I didn't know how to repair it, or to make new connections to the world. Instead, I grabbed at a new identity. Overnight, I became Cain. Cain lived in a vacuum. He was a desert wanderer and fugitive. Wearing his mask saved me. Once I had clasped that mask over my face, I was afraid to take it off. Why? I believed it gave a shape and structure to my features, that if I ever removed it, the real me under its sinister surface would be revealed not as a face but as a single, huge teardrop. If anyone touched that strange, transparent globe, even myself, no matter how lightly, it would burst.

The mask of Cain was structure, was protection against the absolute sense of terror and vulnerability I felt—the terror I felt about living in such a dangerous world. I *wanted* to be Cain, because if I wasn't Cain I was something even more frightening: a twelve-year-old boy who had stood in a field and heard a gun go off and seen a boy fall dead and seen in that same instant the fabric of the world tear from top to bottom like a painted stage set. Behind it, an empty abyss.

At twelve, I had grabbed the mask of Cain. Now, fifteen and back in Germantown, I felt the mask slipping away from me and I sensed I'd need to find new meanings if I were to survive. The meanings I needed had to be commensurate with the terrors I'd seen and felt.

My teachers, almost without exception, meant well. I think they wanted to bring me back inside the social community. But by then, the safe world they espoused—the closed system of multiple choice, vocabulary quiz, essay questions—seemed no more than an elaborate and silly game.

I felt like that man in the Renaissance engraving who's on all fours and has poked his head through the shell of the atmosphere, so that it sticks out into the higher realms where he has a clear view of the heavenly spheres and the glory of the fixed stars. Only my head had poked down *into* the earth and I was gazing now, not at the orderly constellations of a cosmic order, but at the chaos and flames of hell.

35

The Maidens
of Hades

MY SEARCH FOR NEW MEANINGS LED ME TO STRANGE PLACES, among them a store called Lawlor's. Three or four days a week, instead of boarding the school bus at three, I'd walk the half mile up to our town, hang out at Lawlor's for a few hours, then make my way farther up the street to my father's office. There I'd sit on a stool reading in what had been my grandmother's kitchen, waiting until Dad finished up his afternoon office hours around seven in the evening. Somewhere along the line I would have done my homework and we would make our way out toward the old house, stopping for house calls on the way or zooming back for evening hours, depending on the day of the week.

Lawlor's was essentially a soda fountain named after its owners, Ray and Maggie. But it was more than that. It harbored, in its shadowy interior, the whole buried life of the community, all that was suspect and intense. Its stale air buzzed and blared with noise from a pinball machine and a jukebox, those two technologies of the Devil. But it was Lawlor's array of magazines that most alarmed and offended—bright-colored, indisputable proof that a whole world of desire and mystery existed beyond the drear, constricted horizons of our tiny town. *Hot Rod, Popular Mechanics, Men's Adventure, Field and Stream, Custom Car, Motor Trend, True Detective,* and then the girlie magazines: *Adam, Playboy, Dude, Frolic, Escapade,* and half a dozen even more Dionysian others. These were all laid out in neat rows on a large flat shelf in the front window alcove with only their titles showing.

Above the magazines, two large, pivoting racks hung down from the ceiling like long Chinese lanterns: one was stuffed with comics, the other with cheap paperbacks. Between them, they blocked out all light from the street.

I felt safe in Lawlor's. I was too ashamed and self-conscious to move at ease in the daylight world of other people at school. And I could no longer turn to solitude and wandering in the natural world—there had been a time when wandering in the woods had make me feel light and invisible or transparent, but all that had changed with my mother's death. Now, I felt a heaviness filling my body, a shadowy opacity that roiled there and tied itself in knots.

It was not Nature but the Netherworld that called me. Lawlor's darkness was where I felt most at home. It wasn't Hell in any Christian sense, but it did seem to resemble some pagan Underworld inhabited by the dead. It was a claustrophobic place impacted with the same obscure intensities I felt in myself. It was here I belonged—not with the small group around the pinball or the jukebox, but by myself in a booth, with a Coke and a package of Hostess Twinkies reading comics. Or dawdling at the comic rack as if trying to decide between the Classics Illustrated *Jane Eyre* and *Archie* while all the while I could see the titles of the pinup magazines spread out on the flat shelf below and wished only to yank one from its place and leaf through it quickly. Terror and risk and shame! Intensity! This glimpse of a world beyond imagining. This was the mystery that haunted me, women who exposed their breasts and smiled—two magical gestures at the same time, this was the mystery at the heart of it all.

Have I said Lawlor's was the Netherworld? Then Ray Lawlor was no less than Hades himself: large, pale, and enervated, like a giant albino toad or a troll so lost in rolls of fat he could hardly move. He dressed always in a shirt and pants as dark as the grease-coated, varnished paneling that lined the walls, dark almost as the faux-marble counter that reflected back the round moon of his face like a midnight pond. Dark in his dark lair, Ray combed his lank black hair straight across the large white dome of his head and looked out at the world with a mournful, harassed expression. Mostly, he sat at a small desk halfway back along the wall, with a stub of pencil in his hand and another tucked behind his ear, ceaselessly mulling over accounts and scribbling on small sheets of paper, as though being Hades meant he must perpetually puzzle over itemized lists of the dead.

And Maggie, Ray's wife, was Persephone the Maiden—a tiny redhead with a bouffant, a cigarette, and a foul mouth; even with her foot-high, teased hairdo she was under five feet. With her puckered, pouting face, she looked like Mickey Rooney eating a lemon. How old was she? Ageless. She'd hardly changed at all from the day of her abduction—she'd somehow been preserved, pickled in brine, a doll, as if Barbie never grew, but only aged.

To me, Maggie and Ray seemed demonic in their oddness. I chose them now not only as sponsors but almost as surrogate parents for a new birth. I entered their lair, their underworld. I died into it as a skinny, alienated adolescent and was reborn as someone precariously balancing over his own inner abyss on three slender threads. The first thread connected me to comic books. I took them back to my booth and read, one after the other: *Archie, Superman, Green Lantern, Scrooge McDuck.* It didn't matter how dumb or predictable they were. It was as if I were gripped by a nostalgia for childhood, an idiot innocence I'd never possessed. The second thread attached me to the rack of cheap paperbacks, which were mostly mysteries, but here and there a Signet Classic. And so I began to buy and read those "classics." Those serious books helped sustain me for the brief time of reading them. They were like little buoys that kept me afloat on the night sea as long as I read them. But when each book was finished, I began to sink again, to drown.

The third thread connected me to the girlie magazines. How I felt a thrill as I gazed at their smiles and bare breasts, the photos of nymphs in Hades' morgue—the nameless, dead beauties. These were not the famous ones whom François Villon, the medieval poet and criminal, lamented by name in his litany with the refrain "where are the snows of yesteryear." These sad lasses staring up out of the gloom of Lawlor's were anonymous from the start. And yet their smiles seemed to speak of the body's possible joys, of erotic mysteries that they understood and were eager to share. My despair was so deep I might as well have been dead, but as I gazed at these women I felt almost alive, felt a yearning for intimacy and the meaning that might come from it.

36

The Thread
of Poetry

AND THEN, DURING MY SENIOR YEAR IN HIGH SCHOOL,
everything changed. The concentration of bright students in our
class of thirty-six was higher than anyone had seen in years, and the
school authorities had been watching our progress through the
grades with amazement and wonder. Now Mrs. Irving, the school
librarian, stepped forward with a proposal the like of which had
never been heard in Germantown. She would take six of the best students in our class and set up an honors English group that would
meet each day with her in the library while the other kids had their
regular English class.

I had known Mrs. Irving since seventh grade, when I began
going to the upper school library. I knew the library primarily as the
place where flirting could happen. It was only a single room with a
series of tables. There were no stacks you could linger behind, so the
main trick was to arrange to meet a girl there and then sit across
from her at the same table. If things were really intense between the
two of you, you might try actual physical contact under the table,

rubbing your pant leg against her naked shin. Some of the girls wore stockings—and the sensation of that preternatural slipperiness, even through the fabric of my pants, was intoxicating.

I saw Mrs. Irving as most students saw her—as an impediment to powerful urges. From her desk in midroom against the wall of windows, she kept a sharp eye out for any hanky-panky and brought her voice down with the authority of a ruler slapped flat on a desk. Short, stocky, with a severe bob and an alert face that seemed permanently frowning, she was not generally popular.

Our newly established honors English class met in a side room of the library that was used for storage. We also had permission to go into this room during the day to talk. This room was the only place in the school where students were allowed to talk together, the only social space, unless you counted the bathrooms and cafeteria. We were keenly aware of the privilege and enjoyed it immensely.

In the course of that class, the six of us entered worlds we never knew existed before. We traveled the full forty miles north to Albany to see the Royal Canadian Ballet. No one traveled anywhere on school trips from Germantown, other than athletic teams heading off in a bus over backroads to encounter the representatives of some equally forlorn hamlet on its home court. We drove—inconceivable!—the one hundred and twenty miles south to New York City to see a matinee of Chekhov's *The Seagull*. Mrs. Irving drove us to these places—she conceived of these possibilities and had the heroic initiative to get us there. It's not that we'd never been to Albany or New York before, though some hadn't, but that we'd never realized you could go there to specifically seek a cultural experience. And more than that: I saw there were people out there—musicians, performers, artists—who wanted urgently to make and communicate meanings, who devoted energy and skill to intensifying the sense of what it was to be alive. Mrs. Irving showed us that the world was immeasurably bigger and richer and more curious than we had previously been able to imagine, and she showed us there were roads that connected Germantown to this astounding world.

Wonderful as all this was, it wasn't what mattered most. The world that was to lure me and place me under its spell was an inner world, the world inside me. Not the landscape already crisscrossed with roads that are other people's novels or plays, but my own interior landscape. I was enthralled by the possibility of making my own paths out of language, each word put down like a luminous footstep, the sentence itself extending behind me in a white trail and, ahead of me, the dark unknown urging me to explore it.

We kept journals. We did daily writing assignments: descriptive sketches, haiku, book reports, a one-act play, short stories, poems. POEMS! Were there more than a few? I'm not sure, but for me there was a single pivotal experience.

One afternoon, we all took a walk back behind the school across the playing fields. If we were sent out with an assignment in mind, I don't remember it. I think we just all strolled about enjoying the day. We did wander off the school grounds into the nearby scrub woods, maybe only a few hundred yards, to a place where we scrambled on top of a large rock. It felt important to step off the school grounds, to transgress that mental boundary that had ruled my whole life as a student.

When we got back inside, Mrs. Irving asked us all to write something about the walk. I wrote a poem about being alone on a rock by the sea. What I felt while I was writing it was overwhelming. I felt an incredible sense of release. I felt as if the passionate and agonized inner world that I really inhabited was suddenly and precisely given form and objective reality. I had thought writers were supposed to describe the "real" world we all knew, only they used vivid, accurate, interesting language. They would describe the wood grain on the yellow-pine table so precisely you could see it before your eyes, almost palpable. They used language you could test against the world of your own experience. But what I felt when I wrote my first, clumsy poem was that the words were *creating* a world, not describing a preexisting one. I had tapped into the inner world of my emotions and feelings and was trying to give them form in concrete language. In this first poem, I had been lucky enough to find a physical equivalent for my inner state and the emotional experience was joyous.

Those first spider threads I'd thrown out at Lawlor's—those tentative, guilty linkings to the world of books, of childhood nostalgia, of eroticism—were nothing compared to the precious thread of poetry. Once I had hold of it, I knew I might find my way out of the labyrinth of my own consciousness. I was no Theseus. No hero who'd slain the man-eating minotaur raging at the heart of the maze (though I dreamt violent, shadowy dreams where blood was spilled). No Ariadne, loving me passionately, had placed that thread in my hand. I'd simply woken in the dark with the thread of poetry gripped in my fist and—perhaps—the nightmare combat already behind me.

What the myths don't mention is that there is no light in the labyrinth. And that it takes years—it took me years—to get out. Was I going to perish there in the dark? I didn't know for sure. But I did know this: if I once let go of that thread, I would certainly die.

The thread was poetry. True to poetry's laws of dream and metamorphosis, it changed in my hand as I held it. Sometimes, it was the thinnest silk filament, so fine it almost cut my palm simply resting there. Other times, it thickened and became slick as if with blood, all warm and wet, and I felt as if it was my own throbbing guts paid out and now to be followed back toward what source or exit? Other times, it became braided and dry as a rope and I wondered if I were meant to twist it around my neck. Sounds would come from its side where small wound-mouths had opened to utter almost human, almost animal cries. And sometimes it seemed a woman's hair as impossibly long and fragrant as Rapunzel's.

This was poetry, not poems. Poems are discrete artifacts of language that prove someone's imagination and linguistic gifts have triumphed over disorder in a definitive, shaped way. What I held onto then was not poems, but the idea of poetry—which I had to follow for years before I emerged into the light, before I could let go of the thread for a moment and sit down to write my first poem.

37

The Excursion

MY FIRST, OVERWHELMING MOTIVE FOR TRYING TO WRITE poems was to escape from my sense of shame and misery into another world. I also tried escaping in a more mundane way: by skipping school and running away.

A hitchhiker's thumb pointed over the bridge and up toward the Catskills. A knapsack with two cans of creamed corn and one of Del Monte fruit cocktail. (I forgot a can opener and tried, unsuccessfully, to bang them open with a rock.) Sleeping in fields, making my bug-bitten way to the little village of Woodstock, where I found something that struck me with the power of revelation: a recruiting poster for the Kingston chapter of CORE, the Congress of Racial Equality. It showed a photo of three young people, two black and one white, arms linked and singing. The photo reminded me of Deschapelles, that little boat of light on the tennis court where the Haitian and American workers sang hymns, rowing with their voices through the deep Haitian night. It also reminded me of my mother's idealism and how, because of it, I'd had experiences even before Haiti that made this picture engaging to me.

Most of the orchards around Germantown were small, family-run operations, but some were large enough to be tied into the migrant labor system. Each summer, busloads of black agricultural workers would arrive to harvest the fruit, having followed the growing season up the Atlantic coast from Florida. A farmer would contract with a crew boss who owned a bus he'd fill with workers and, on a pre-arranged day, he'd deliver his workers to pick the ripe crop. The crew boss got money from the farmer for delivering his workers as well as a cut from the pickers' paychecks. Men, women, and children, they'd move through the orchards picking cherries (the crop I knew) six days a week from dawn to dark.

The pickers lived in shack camps deep in the orchards. It was a grim, hopeless life in most ways—the pickers were at the mercy of both farmer and crew boss and there was no way out of their impoverished lives or their dismal camps. The camps had no electricity or plumbing and were built way back in the orchards so they were far from prying eyes. On rare occasions, you might see a picker trudging the highway in search of some grocery store miles and miles away, but that was foolish—wasting picking time when, for only twice its real cost, you could buy it from the crew boss or the orchard owner's son. I'd seen some of the camps on house calls with my father, the farmer meeting us at road's edge on his tractor to guide us back through the maze of orchard roads to a cluster of shacks. The dark trees pressing in on the one-room, tar-papered huts; the sound of loud music from transistor radios and the sweet smell of muscatel and cheap booze mingling with a thick odor of fried food and kerosene. Dad was usually there to sew someone up after a knife fight. And once, I saw a scorched fingerbone pointing skyward from a smoldering heap of ash and twisted tin as if the dead man was indicating his last wish was to go to heaven, having seen enough of hell in his life on earth.

But I saw another side of this world also. It was Mom's idea that I should work in an orchard and know something of that labor if not that life. When I was thirteen, she lied about my age to local officials to get me working papers. She dropped me off each morning at 6 A.M. and picked me up, exhausted, at five each night by the sorting barn. I was the only white picker in the orchard, the only local kid. Probably, the farmer had hired me as a favor to my parents.

There were problems. I was sent out with the men to pick the full-sized trees, but I was scrawny and barely five feet tall. If I got the balance point, I could lift my twelve-foot oak ladder off the ground, but I couldn't heft it straight up into the high branches where it needed to be. At best, on my own, I could get it sloped six feet up into the lowest branches at an absurdly acute angle to the ground. Every twenty minutes or so, one or another of the pickers would appear at the foot of my ladder, tell me to get down and then grab it and fling it up among the unpicked branches in another part of the tree. These movements with the ladder were a brusque and efficient ballet, but something about the way they were done gave me a sense of tolerant goodwill and my gratitude was boundless. Not even I, with my enormous self-consciousness and insecurity, could interpret the speed with which this deed was done as being unfriendly—everyone moved all day with as much celerity as they could. Your whole life was thirty-five cents per five-gallon pail; no one wasted a single moment or movement.

Except when you were up among the branches full of bright fruit, with your ladder securely braced and the bucket hanging by a hook from your belt and already filling with ripe red globes you pulled in with both hands. Then you might—if you were one of the crew, not me—let your mind and tongue loose and join in the continuous flow of gossip, razzing, and opinion that went on all day across the rows. The debate about who was the true king of the twist, Fats Domino or Chubby Checker, led to some of the most hilarious and inventive metaphors and obscenities. There were times I had to hold onto my ladder with both hands to keep from falling off in a fit of laughter. I loved that river of talk. Its fluid grace, its dense rhythms and calculated, self-delighting alterations of pitch seemed almost Shakespearean and a million miles away from the flat, joyless voices I'd grown up among.

I made my way down from Woodstock to Kingston and searched out the address on the poster. When at last I found it, it was a storefront building, locked, but with a sign in the window announcing that the organization met each Saturday afternoon.

Late that evening, I learned I couldn't cross the Kingston bridge on foot and so called home. When Inga fetched me an hour later at the toll booth, she seemed pleased:

"Boy, are you in for it now, buster. Your father is furious and when he gets home tonight you're really going to get it."

But Dad wasn't much of a disciplinarian, and he must himself have been intrigued by my adventure and discovery, because that Saturday he let me borrow a car and drive the thirty miles to Kingston to investigate.

What I found was about a dozen people in a bare room with thirty folding chairs and a table. The chapter president was a black politician named Eustice Smith. His wife and teenage son and daughter were also members—his wife, the treasurer; his son, the vice president. There were several other local black citizens as well and a white couple from Woodstock. The white man was a painter named David Ruff. He was a hunchbacked dwarf with a thatch of thick black hair he kept brushing aside to show a serious face that would periodically break into a wide, reassuring grin. His wife was a poet named Holly Bye.

I sat through the meeting, which had already begun before I arrived. When it was over, I did the best I could to satisfy people's curiosity about who I was and why I was there, but since I didn't know myself, my answers were probably odd. The truth was the Civil Rights Movement was one more thread I hoped would reconnect me to the world of meaning.

The next week, our group canvassed voters in the black wards. I did my awkward best, knocking on doors, asking questions from a list we'd prepared hoping to gauge what support there was for political change. As the weeks went by, it became clear that our tiny chapter was deeply divided. According to the Smiths, we should be focused on local issues only, but David and Holly felt we should be paying more attention to our links with the national headquarters and issues that went beyond the local. I found this constant infighting confusing. I had felt relieved and proud to have made my choice to join this group. I thought we were all on the same side and believed the same important things. Now, the simple clarity and significance of my choice was being thrown into question by arguments and personality clashes.

In the middle of the summer, David called with the news that CORE was sponsoring a demonstration at the Democratic National Convention in Atlantic City. The goal was to support the Mississippi Freedom Democratic Party delegates in their bid to unseat the regular, all-white, racist Mississippi delegation which had been elected under rules that excluded all black voters. By such confrontations at the national level, CORE hoped to keep the pressure for political change in the Democratic Party high. Lyndon Johnson had done some hurried backroom deals with most of the other civil rights groups—promising them quick legislative action, if they promised not to embarrass him at the convention in Atlantic City. Only CORE refused the offer, and so a busload of its members came out from New York City and one lone car with six of us crammed inside wended its way down the Hudson Valley and out over the Pine Barrens toward the ocean.

I knew nothing of the larger political picture then. I was seventeen and I was very excited to be headed for my first demonstration. David and Holly, myself, John and Fred, two young black men from Kingston, and a white girl only a few years older than me from Woodstock—all jammed into David's old Chevy. The girl, whom I hadn't met before, had long, dark hair and seemed to me very beautiful and exotic.

Atlantic City was gray and tawdry back in 1964, long before the glitz of gambling threw a neon facade over its decay. What I remember of the city is that small area of the ramshackle boardwalk our group had staked out in front of the convention center—a space where twenty-five or so of us walked around and around in a large oval. We each carried placards referring to the Freedom Democratic Party delegation and such classic slogans as "One Man, One Vote." There were also three large charcoal portraits of Andrew Goodman, James Chaney, and Michael Schwerner, the young civil rights workers who had been murdered by the Klan and whose bodies had just been found.

I was surprised at how hostile people were in the crowd that surrounded us on the boardwalk. I constantly heard violent taunts and insults and was actually afraid. But amazed, too; startled that well-dressed, normal-looking men and women could say such vile things, could twist their faces into such angry and vicious grimaces. I hadn't realized how deep and violent racial hatreds were.

Yet all this came to me as if from a great distance, because I had fallen under the spell of those three faces floating high above the other posters. A few months before, when they had disappeared in a car last seen near Philadelphia, Mississippi, they had been three mortal young men, not utterly unlike me. Something had happened to them in Mississippi. They had died there—killed by Klan members colluding with a local sheriff—and their bodies had been secretly bulldozed into a red clay dam. But after their bodies had been discovered, they were resurrected here on the boardwalk in these giant portraits larger than life. Their deaths had transformed them into something high and noble. When Peter died, I had experienced death in its most violent and mysterious form. It had hit with the inexplicable and implacable suddenness of a lightning bolt. That bolt opened a crack in the field where Peter fell. Not a huge crack, but it went down forever. It was an abyss that opened and swallowed someone I loved. Did anyone else even see it? They saw the dead child. They lifted the dead child's body up and brought it out of the field, but did they see that crack that opened in the earth and swallowed his soul and my soul also?

When that crack opened in the field, I shouted or cried out in agony: "What does it mean?" I needed an answer as deep as that crack. But no answer could come out of that fissure, that wound in the field because no one was down there: not God, not the Devil, not Charley Hayes or Peter, no one. There was no one down there at the bottomless bottom of that crack and so no response could originate from it.

But at that moment in Atlantic City, I thought I heard an answer. It said: "Blood for blood." Expiation, atonement. To become a martyr for something truly noble. Chaney, Schwerner, Goodman. The Protestant religion I was raised in didn't have martyrs, or confession (how I would have loved to confess so that I might be forgiven); it didn't have Christ's body writhing in agony on the cross (how I could have related to that suffering). The ascetic church I had sporadically attended in childhood was bare of any images I could relate to; images that could mediate between me and the Abyss. Images that could carry meanings to me out of the Abyss, the crack in the field.

When I saw those three huge charcoal faces floating above us in Atlantic City, I felt I had found at last believable images, images radiant with significance. Goodman, Chaney, Schwerner. Their calm faces, their gazes clear and at peace. Selves that were mortal and yet had gone beyond their mortality and had risen above their bodies. These three young men had been lifted up into meaning.

I thought: if I can *become* them—if I, too, can act and be caught up in history. If I, too, can become a heroic martyr. Trudging in a circle with a slogan on a placard wouldn't work, nor canvassing neighborhoods with questionnaires. To redeem myself for something as terrible as Peter's death and my mother's death, I would need something transformative, something that would change me forever. This all took place in Atlantic City in 1964, the summer when the full power of young, white, middle-class idealism was being tapped by the Movement, especially SNCC and CORE. "Freedom Summer," when 650 white middle-class kids from all over the country descended on Mississippi and the Deep South as volunteers. But I was only seventeen then—a minor. I wasn't old enough to go. I'd have to wait, impatiently, for next summer and another chance.

38

College

HAMILTON WAS AN ALL-MALE SCHOOL IN A TINY VILLAGE ten miles outside the upstate city of Utica, New York. What was I doing at a school whose two most famous alums were Ezra Pound and B. F. Skinner? A poet so politically reactionary and obtuse, they'd had to try him for treason after the Second World War and he'd only escaped through an insanity plea. And a psychologist who felt that all he had to do to plumb the mysteries of human behavior was extrapolate from the actions of caged rats given food pellets and electric shocks.

I knew I hated the school for a hundred reasons the first week I was there. Many disaffected freshmen marched blithely down a path of self-destruction and flunked out by the first semester's end. I loathed the place, but I studied sporadically and, thanks partly to Dad's jug of amphetamines, crammed efficiently enough at finals to do well. The only class I loved was ancient civilization, taught by a passionate, timid eccentric named Herbert Long. Bespectacled and bow-tied, Herbie would drone on in his nasal whine about the Greeks: "Gentlemen, *sophrosyne* was the essential Greek concept for safe living. 'Moderation in all things.'" But Herbie's love and knowledge of his subject was far from moderate, and the Greek tragedians he introduced us to were fascinated by human passions. I could relate to Aeschylus and the others: agony and violence in families, children sacrificed on bloody altars, obscure curses flowing through a lineage from generation to generation. What must have seemed archaic or hysterical to many of my classmates seemed to me matter-of-fact tales of family dynamics.

Alienated from the social and academic world of the college, I spent many afternoons on long walks in the woods and fields adjacent to the campus. These were solitary excursions that extended for hours, melancholy cousins of my childhood walks along the ditch or my later expeditions into the woods with my rifle before Peter's death. Only now I lacked the joyous, outer-directed intensity and sense of purpose that the search for turtles had given me, or even the gun which had always implied more purpose than I really had.

Now, I wandered with pieces of folded paper and a pen in my coat pocket. I still took pleasure in the walking itself and in periodically stopping to carefully study something that seemed of interest: a spider's web or some vista from a ridge. But for all of my lingering to stare intently at a wren's nest in a leafless November alder bush, it wasn't the wonders of nature that mattered to me anymore, but my own inchoate confusions and loneliness. I still held to nature as somehow a possible answer to this anguish, but the natural world seldom had the power to take me out of myself as it had once, to make me lose my sense of self in marveling at some event or object. Now my only hope had to do with the pen and paper in my pocket and with the words I wrote there as I sat in a field or leaned against a tree.

Many of my new heroes were poets, the young Yeats and Dylan Thomas especially. When I read the early poems of Yeats—the lonely, melancholic Yeats pining for a "beloved"—I wept. I was amazed that the words of someone long dead could affect me so. I wanted to be able to do that: to move someone with my words. And so I entered the dream of lyric poets: the dream that black scratchings on a white page can cross the huge abyss between humans, that a stranger can lift up that page years later or hundreds of miles away and be moved, troubled and brought alive by words you put there.

Both Thomas and Yeats had fused their feelings with the natural world. I found pictures of them and other poets in magazines, cut them out and pasted them to my dormitory wall. On the inside of my window shade I had written in large red letters the final lines of Thomas's "Fern Hill"—"Time held me green and dying / Though I sang in my chains like the sea."

I still hoped the transaction with poetry could be between the natural world and me, that I could somehow become a "nature poet" and be spared the need to concern my poems with other people and with the enormous confusions I felt around them, or the intolerable sense of guilt and despair that being close to them stirred up inside me. I thought perhaps if I could write poems about the natural world that were beautiful, this might be both a relief for me personally and also something that might redeem me in the eyes of others.

When I discovered the poems of the Austrian Expressionist Georg Trakl, I felt an almost shocking sense of kinship. This sense was heightened by the uncanny fact that he and I were both born on February 3, he exactly seventy years before me. Trakl was haunted by obscure family guilts and addicted to various drugs. He died at twenty-seven, committing suicide in the aftermath of a particularly bloody battle in World War I when he had been left in charge of a barnful of wounded and dying soldiers. I identified with Trakl's dream-saturated, cryptic lyrics and with the hugeness of his alienation.

When Trakl was leaving for the front, he slipped a short note to an acquaintance on the train platform. All it said was: "That the poems might be a partial atonement."

When I could, I fled the campus entirely, finding a ride with someone, or else making my way to the New York State Thruway

entrance and hitching the five hours to New York City. Much as the
big city scared me, I wanted to go there to visit Bob Melnik. I'd first
met Bob when I was sixteen and working as a dishwasher at a summer camp where Bob was a counselor's assistant. In the course of
befriending me that summer, Bob had introduced me to the first
record, just released, of his favorite singer, Bob Dylan. The music,
and much else Melnik was enthusiastic about, was way outside what
I could understand or appreciate at the time, but that following fall
I had taken Mrs. Irving's class and what I'd been introduced to there
made me eager to become reacquainted with Melnik and find out
what more he could show me. So, one summer evening after my
senior year, I invited Melnik and some fellow counselors to visit me
at the old house. We lit a bonfire down by the stream and drank
beer and talked. Bob introduced me to a counselor named Devi.
She had a wide, full mouth and deep-set eyes. Every once in a while,
she'd tuck her chin down so that her straight hair fell forward on
either side of her face and then she'd stare up at me through the
parting as if through a waterfall and smile quietly. I found the gesture
enthralling. At midnight I was in their car headed back to the camp
with them. Devi had infirmary duty, which meant staying the night
in a small cabin with a bunkbed and no patients. We lay together on
the narrow mattress and made out passionately. All the girls I'd
dated in Germantown seemed to have signed a secret pact that
meant they were not allowed to respond or even move when a boy
kissed them or put his arms around them. Devi was different. She
touched me in places I'd never dared touch myself. She made small
noises like a happy animal. When I left that night, I was still a virgin, but I had felt sensations that told me there were whole worlds
hidden in this mystery of sex.

That fall, I hitched down from Hamilton to visit Melnik and
met Devi again. She, Melnik, and I went together to a party.
Afterward, she and I made out in Riverside Park until 2 A.M., when
I returned to my fleabag hotel. Early the next morning there was a

knock at my door. I answered dressed in underpants. Devi was standing there, soaked from a morning rainstorm. Then we were naked on the bed, making love. And then it was over and Devi fell asleep. I got up and sat on the chair by the window looking out and trying to make sense of the experience.

My whole body seemed beautiful, because she had moved her hands across it, caressed it, as I had caressed her body. It's as if that touch was a consecration, not the touch alone, but the stroking movement across skin. I was dazed and joyous for hours. I gazed out over the gray October cityscape of buildings in the drizzle.

Devi slept. I sat by the window. My body felt whole and empty like a shell the sea has scoured clean and washed up on a beach. I felt at peace with myself, at peace in myself.

When she woke, she left. What happened between us wasn't the beginning of a relationship. I may have failed to respond in the way she needed or wanted; I may have been unable to speak. She may have had other plans. I don't know. But what I do know is that what happened between us was amazing to me: I felt that we had knelt together in the same place, at the same shadowy shrine. She brought her mysterious longings and needs and I brought mine. We exchanged them as offerings. But we hardly spoke.

All through my freshman year—through classes and all-night study sessions, through romances and poetic efforts—I continued to be haunted by the posters of Goodman, Schwerner, and Chaney I had seen at the Democratic National Convention. As I moved out into the larger world, history seemed like it might be one of the meanings that would sustain me. History whose mode is action, whose defining mark is the decisive deed, and whose pages are spattered with the blood of martyrs.

I still might not have made the leap into political action if it hadn't been for a movie I saw that spring. It was a black-and-white documentary on the Spanish Civil War called *To Die in Madrid*. Its title derived from the final rallying cry of the Spanish Republicans—a summons to a last, fatal rendezvous when all hope of victory was lost and Franco's triumphant Fascist armies were closing for the decisive battle that would end the war.

Certainly the overall political idealism of the doomed Spanish Republicans moved me. But more than that I was hooked by two particular scenes that seemed to fuse all my preoccupations—writing, history, idealism, martyrdom—into focused moments of coherent drama. In the first, the screen image showed a hillside olive grove—nothing but the trees themselves with their ancient trunks contorted like human bodies holding improbable poses and their bright leaves glittering in the sun. While we watched these trees, a voice recited Federico Garcia Lorca's "Somnambule Ballad":

> Green, how I want you green.
> Green wind. green branches.
> The ship upon the sea
> and the horse in the mountain.

A high, wild wind began to move through the olive trees, thrashing their branches into a frenzied dance as another voice told how a squad of Franco's soldiers had abducted Lorca, taken him out on a lonely road, and murdered him. I was stunned at the beauty and sadness of it all.

The other scene focused on Miguel de Unamuno, the great philosopher and writer, who was in his seventies when the war broke out. He was rector of the University of Salamanca in an area that had quickly fallen to Franco's forces. One day, the Fascists commandeered his university for a rally and forced Unamuno to sit on the speaker's stand along with prominent Fascist politicians and military leaders. In one speech, a one-armed general led the crowd in a chant of "Long Live Death." When the crowd had calmed down, Unamuno stood up and denounced the general's nihilism, an act of courage that sent him to prison.

Here were literary heroes who had also become political heroes through risk and martyrdom! Granted, Garcia Lorca and Unamuno had spent long years learning their respective arts—they had not gone simply from mortal to martyr, but had fulfilled a transitional identity that I too longed for: poet. In *To Die in Madrid* I saw writers who also became heroes. Maybe I could do the same. What did it matter if I were a real poet yet or not? I heard the stirring summons of the movie's title calling all idealists to take a final stand: to die in Madrid. If I wished to be part of a great historical drama, and perhaps also to become a hero or martyr of that drama, then this was my chance.

When I left the movie theater, it was settled. I would go south as a volunteer activist. I would become a full-time political organizer.

And so I set in motion the process that would have me, in the spring of 1965, at the age of eighteen, heading to Mississippi as a volunteer. How I filled out the forms I don't know. I must have written more than one letter to a committee at SNCC, the Student Nonviolent Coordinating Committee that was organizing the project. I must have filled out some application forms—yet I remember nothing of the prelude to my journey, nothing except my father's offer to buy me a car to get there. It was a 1957 brown-and-white Ford. If I hadn't had a car, I would have taken a bus, but the car gave me freedom and mobility. I'd never even driven over a state line, and now I was going to journey alone a thousand miles into an unknown part of the country. According to SNCC instructions, I had my long hair cut short and assembled a wardrobe of innocuous khaki pants and short-sleeved shirts. Finally, on the morning I began my journey, I received what had become Dad's traditional parting gift—a travel-sized bottle of amphetamine.

39

Aftermath

IT WAS LATE AUGUST OF 1965. I'D BEEN BACK FROM THE South over a month now. I was standing on the ledge of a window eight stories above West End Avenue in New York City. It was one of those large windows where the upper half slides down, so that I had to climb over the lower half to get out onto the ledge itself. I stood there holding onto the top of the window frame and staring down into the midnight street. Keith Devins, a friend from Hamilton, had left about twenty minutes before. He had brought some grass and I'd gotten stoned for what was only the second or third time in my life. We had talked a bit, but mostly I sank into myself. And now I was standing on the ledge looking down and trying to get some message from inside. I could see what I was doing—I could even feel what I was doing in a very numb sense—but I couldn't feel what I was feeling.

I wasn't out on the ledge for the breeze, though that felt good—balmy and laden with the rich night smells of New York in summer. I was there waiting to step off, to let go my hold on the window as if I were only hesitating on the bank of a tropical river at night—almost ready to ease myself into its welcoming strangeness, just lingering there enjoying the fragrances, the soft wind, the lights. Hesitating, with all my senses turned outward, but trying also, trying desperately to hear something from inside.

Earlier in the week, I'd been about to cross Eighth Avenue when I heard a shout close behind me. A young man in a T-shirt ran past me and out into the street. I heard a sharp sound and the running man fell face down flat on the pavement.

On the cover of the *Daily News* the next morning, that same man, in the same spot, filled the whole front page. The photographer must have been standing exactly where I was at almost the identical moment. And the dead man? Someone who'd tried to steal a car from a parking lot; someone who'd been shot by someone who must also have been standing almost where I stood. One more no one whose life was extinguished, and yet his image was reproduced a million times on every cover of the *News*. For that one day, he was everywhere and millions of people saw him (saw, really, his anonymous corpse). Then he was gone: folded and tossed in wastebaskets, abandoned on park benches or dropped to the floor of subway cars, lifting and falling in the hot gusts that funneled through alleys. His image on the front page was like a mockery of those posters of Goodman, Chaney, and Schwerner and all the hope I had placed in them.

Up on the ledge high above the street, I had a sense of unreality. I no longer knew who I was. For all I could tell now I was the man with the camera who'd taken that photo. Or perhaps the man with the gun who had so casually shot a fleeing person in the back. Or the would-be thief himself, so still and at peace in the street, as I would be if I stepped off the ledge. Or the bystander who saw it all, the kid alone in the city, numb with fear and loneliness.

That same week, the week of August 22, 1965, I had opened another newspaper. This time it was the *New York Times*. In it, I saw a photograph of someone I recognized. His name was Lester Smallman. He was a native of Hayneville, Alabama, and the previous afternoon he had shotgunned a seminary student to death in broad daylight outside a grocery store in that tiny, rural town surrounded by swamps.

I knew him because two months earlier, in late June of that same summer, he and another man had stopped my car on Route 80 between Selma and Montgomery. I want to say they arrested me, but kidnapped would be more accurate, or abducted at gunpoint, since neither of them was a law officer and I had committed no crime. That didn't stop them from announcing they intended to kill me.

The point-blank shotgun blast with which Smallman killed the seminary student was meant for someone else: a pregnant black woman standing next to him. At the last moment, the unarmed student pushed the woman aside and was shot full in the stomach. At the subsequent trial, held in a courthouse only two hundred yards from the murder site itself, a local jury found the killer innocent by reason of self-defense.

Apparently Smallman was angry because the Federal Voting Rights Act had recently been passed. He wanted to do something about it, protest in some way. I've often thought how lucky I was that the law hadn't been enacted two months earlier, when I was jailed in that town. Like me, the woman, the student, and others had been held in the Hayneville jail for a week without charges; like me, they'd been released suddenly on their own recognizance. Unlike me, they had no way to get out of town quickly. They spent a desperate few hours trying to find transportation to Montgomery, but had no luck. Meanwhile, the killer's sense of frustration was rising toward explosive action.

And so it happened.

This little story seems partly inevitable, partly pure random coincidence. Local black people are afraid to drive them to Montgomery—there would be consequences; they would pay a price for meddling. The armed man is angry. He is, the *Times* tells us, the son of a prominent local family—perhaps he knows that status confers a kind of immunity on his acts. And at the last second, the student pushed the woman aside.

The death of the car thief before my eyes in the New York City streets was like a punctuation point of emphasis: here's a human life. See it snuffed out before your very eyes and the pedestrian traffic barely pauses. Nothing remarkable here, folks, just keep moving. And then, when I saw Smallman's photo in the *Times,* I couldn't keep moving. It all caught up with me and I stopped moving. I stopped and stood on that window ledge high above West End Avenue. How long did I stand there? Ten minutes? An hour? An eternity? I still can't go near the edges of cliffs, no matter how great the view, because I can still feel the temptation to step off. I know that I could choose to let go of the windowsill, step off the cliff. And if I did, the suspense and vulnerability would be over. Of course, I don't want to die. I love being alive. But the terror of my own vulnerability from that summer still haunts me, and when it combines with my grief and shame over Peter's death, then large, destructive forces inside me assert themselves.

In history, timing is everything. And without my knowing it, the time had passed when the death of a white civil rights worker would have any significant political or social impact. The laws the Movement sought were mostly passed by then. The solidarity between young white and black activists was over. The Watts riots loomed on the horizon. History's gaze had shifted away from the intractable problems in the South and become briefly mesmerized by urban ghetto flames and dark whispers out of Asia.

What awaited me, as I drove alone to Mississippi at the age of eighteen, wasn't history with a large H and my name in bold letters.

It was just the daily grinding of history's great clock, whose gears sometimes mesh smoothly and harmlessly, sometimes catch your sleeve and drag you into the machinery—but always without pausing, without losing the perfect mechanical sequencing that mocks our humanness, mocks both our suffering and our aspirations.

40

Mississippi

MOST OF THE JOURNEY DOWN HAD BEEN UNEVENTFUL. I slept in rest areas and parking lots of large motels. The car broke down once outside Opelika, Georgia, and it took most of an afternoon to get fixed. I got lost in the middle of the night on a backroads detour just over the border into Alabama. When I got to Montgomery, I stopped near the state capitol to look around. The Selma march and its violent end with the murder of Viola Liuzzo, a mother from Detroit, had occurred only a few months before. I pondered with teenage irony the fact that the state police headquarters across from the capitol building was called the "Department of Public Safety." And I drove on, down to Mobile on the Gulf of Mexico.

To allay any unfriendly suspicions on the journey, I had a cover story. I was going to visit my older brother, Bill, at the Air Force base in Biloxi, Mississippi. In fact, he was stationed there at the time, and I did stop to visit briefly on my way down. He'd been having his own encounters with the racial story in the South. A few weeks before, he and some buddies had visited New Orleans. They attended a racially mixed party there and were busted by the police, eliciting a stern warning from the base commander to honor local customs.

I drove on to Waveland, a small gulfside town where SNCC had a rendezvous house down by the water. Here my amnesia sets in for a while. I can't turn to any documents on the Movement to say how many of us Northern volunteers gathered there—the previous summer (known forever as "Freedom Summer") there were more than six hundred, but my year was the aftermath. It earned no historical nickname, and its volunteers were fewer by far. From the outset, there was an edge to our orientation. Again and again, we were told that the new lesson was that local people—both leaders and volunteers—had to spearhead all initiatives. We out-of-state volunteers were only there to do support work and run errands or, at most, respond to local requests.

A few days later, we drove inland to a rural church where we slept on the floors and went through more orientation meetings and got our assignments. I and a tall, thin college kid named Jim from Pittsburgh were to report to the SNCC office in Cleveland, the county seat of Bolivar County up in the Delta region. We were to help out with the cotton strike there. At that time, the pay for chopping weeds in the fields was four dollars a day, dawn to dusk. Men, women, and children worked in brutal heat with "short hoes" that forced them to bend over at painful angles. It was only a matter of a few more years before the picking and cultivating machines would be perfected—everyone knew that. Once that happened, almost all the black agricultural jobs would disappear. Nevertheless, the plan of the moment was to try to organize an effective strike for a decent wage.

When Jim and I pulled up to the house that was SNCC headquarters in Cleveland, a barefoot, bearded, redheaded guy came to the front door. It was like the scene in the movies where the new recruit replacements meet the grizzled, battle-worn sergeant for the first time in the frontline trenches. We must have looked scrubbed and silly to him; he was a bit of a shock to us. Well, he reckoned they'd make what use they could of us, and my car would come in handy.

But we were only there a day or two when word came from Jackson that the governor was trying to push through legislation that would be a major setback for the Movement in Mississippi. Our only hope was the power of negative publicity. The governor wanted a quick and quiet passage, so he had called a secret session of the legislature. Our leaders wanted to stage a mass demonstration in Jackson—the more attention we could focus on the proposed legislation, especially national media attention, the better our chance of scuttling it.

Jim and I had a job to do. The orders were to bring in as many demonstrators as possible. We were sent to rally people and persuade them to make the long and possibly hazardous journey to Jackson. I remember speaking one evening to a small gathering of mostly elderly people in a tiny shack-church in the black hamlet of Beulah. Part of me wants to say that circumstances forced a leadership role on me that night—that I had no choice but to speak and do my best to persuade my rural listeners to respond to this mysterious summons. But that's a little grand. What happened is that either Jim or I had to talk, they were waiting. Jim was probably as shy as I was, and I cracked under the pressure first. There weren't more than a dozen people there, most of them older women wearing the dresses they would have worn to church on Sunday. I said my piece as best I could, relaying what information I'd been given, but I felt awkward and foreign. I sat down and the small congregation gazed at me in silence. Finally, a tiny, ancient woman in a blue-print dress and crow-wing hat got up and said: "Well, it seems to me that these nice boys have traveled an awfully long way to see us, and the least we can do is show them a little hospitality." She then went on to speak simply and persuasively about what they could do, and what they *needed* to do, and what the Good Lord wanted them to do. She only spoke briefly, but when she sat emphatically back down, she did so to murmurs of "Amen, amen."

Before Jim and I left Beulah that evening, we walked down its single dirt street and took a path that led to the Mississippi. Beulah was nestled up against the river and it seemed like this might be my only chance to see it. As we climbed the steep grassy slope of the levee that kept the river back, its lumbering, freight-train sound grew steadily louder. From the levee's top, we gazed down into darkness. It was there, I could smell it, hear it, feel its movement—the cool, wide expanse of it stretching out into the dark for a mile or more and all of it swirling ceaselessly toward the gulf. But for all its huge force it was invisible on this moonless, overcast night only a cool tang in our nostrils, a breeze on our faces and an immense, relentless, unintelligible roar.

41

Jackson

OUR CONTINGENT LEFT THE NEXT DAWN. WE HAD TWO flatbed trucks crowded with people, my Ford, and another car following along behind. We arrived in Jackson midmorning and got our marching orders.

We must have been about two hundred strong, three-quarters Mississippians, the rest SNCC or CORE volunteers. At least half were women, and there were children as young as six or seven marching with their mothers. I remember more excitement than fear. I felt what must reassure most soldiers on the brink of combat: there were so many of us that we would be safe. Also, it was a clear, sunny day, and our ambition seemed so modest: a peaceful march to the state capitol building.

A clean-cut, young black man from Jackson headquarters approached our Bolivar County contingent where it was gathered in a loose, nervous group alongside one of the trucks in the assembly parking lot.

"OK, listen up. We've been denied a permit to parade. Now, we expected that, that means we can't walk in the street. So, here's what we're going to do. We're going to move out in pairs, five feet apart on the sidewalks. Stop for traffic lights. The police chief has let us know that we will be arrested at some point, so if you aren't ready for that, now's the time to get out. Any questions?"

"Are we supposed to cooperate with the arrest?"

"Absolutely. Don't mess around here and everything should be pretty peaceful. We've got pretty good media coverage here. There are a lot of cameras watching this, so there shouldn't be any rough stuff. No one should get hurt."

"What about going limp?" asked a veteran. That was the technique of passively resisting arrest by collapsing loose-limbed on the sidewalk and forcing them to use at least two officers to lift you bodily into the paddywagon. It was a nonviolent way of slowing the whole process down.

"We don't recommend it," the young man answered. "You might get roughed up a bit. But it's your own decision."

We lined up in pairs on the sidewalk and began moving out around 11 A.M. We'd gone a quarter mile or so when everyone halted and we heard that arrests had begun at the head of the line. As my turn to be arrested approached, what I saw reassured me. Everything seemed very peaceful, even courteous. True, there were at least twenty officers there, but there must have been a dozen reporters with cameras and several TV crews as well, and they were filming the whole encounter.

Even someone as naive as myself knew that the national media was our best protection against police violence. One major dimension of the civil rights struggle was a complicated, three-way dance between the Movement, local police, and the national media. When police beat unarmed demonstrators, it was an extremely effective way of quelling local enthusiasm for change, but when that same violence was broadcast as "news" on national television, the whole dynamic shifted. People in other parts of the country were shocked and upset to see unarmed citizens beaten with clubs by policemen or attacked by police dogs. It was partly with this in mind that the

Movement screened its volunteers carefully. They sought as many middle-class and upper-middle-class kids as possible, preferably from Ivy League colleges. You didn't have to be a genius to know that Northern whites responded differently when the person being clubbed on their TV screen was a young white girl from the North rather than a local black citizen.

Although I didn't realize until many years later that we volunteers had been carefully chosen for social connections, I certainly understood that at one level we were seen as cannon fodder. Even in the few weeks I'd been in Mississippi, I'd gotten used to the pervasive uneasiness and risks of simply being there—the cars with two-way radio antennae that followed us everywhere, the pickups with gunracks that tailgated us over the back roads. But this was my first experience of marching into the mouths of the cannons and the cameras.

When I and the black man next to me got to the police grouping, an officer recited his memorized phrase: "You are parading without a permit. By order of the city of Jackson, I order you to disperse. Will you do so?" At that point, my heart was beating like crazy and my mouth was so dry I couldn't have spoken. But I stood my ground. Our leaders wanted as many as possible of us to go to jail in the hope that we could halt the system by overwhelming the local jails with more prisoners than they could handle. Still, a number of our demonstrators were rural folk with jobs and families to get back to, and they stepped aside at the officer's challenge.

Those of us who stayed still were taken under each arm by city policemen, and firmly but not roughly led to the curb and up a ramp into a large, closed truck. My memory says that they were painted orange and bore the logo of the Department of Sanitation, but they weren't garbage trucks exactly, merely large closed trucks like the biggest U-Hauls. Those demonstrators who went limp made a slightly more complicated event of the procedure, but the whole process, duly recorded on news cameras, was very straightforward.

When the truck was stuffed with all the standing people it could hold, twenty or so, the doors were slammed shut and locked from the outside. As we pulled away from the curb, we could hear the sirens of a motorcycle escort. We traveled for about fifteen minutes at a slow speed, never stopping, our escort apparently guiding us straight through red lights. There was a good deal of lurching about and jostling in the packed, airless dark of the truck, but no one spoke much and no one could see anything out the few cracks where light leaked in.

At last, our truck stopped and a few minutes later we heard someone setting up a ramp and unbolting the doors. It wasn't the city jail we saw, once our eyes had adjusted to the flood of light streaming in. It was a mob of state highway patrol officers. There must have been sixty of them in a rough semicircle around the open doors of our truck. Every one of them was wearing a motorcycle officer's helmet and mirrored sunglasses. Every one—this was a later perception, learned only at intimate distance—had his badge covered over with black tape so that the identifying number was concealed. Each had his nightstick out and held before him in both hands. Some tapped the thick wooden stick rhythmically against the palm of their free hand, others gripped it as if it were a rifle and they were presenting arms. It seemed, too, that each and every one of them was grinning from ear to ear.

This was our surprise. This was the joker in the deck. None of us would emerge from the truck, so five or six officers came up and grabbed people by an arm or leg and dragged them out. As soon as we reached the ground, they began clubbing us. I can't say how long it went on. It had a kind of leisurely, festive feel about it on their part. They were obviously pleased with the shocked expressions on our faces—remember, we were women and kids, people from ten up to seventy. Our response as the doors flew open made the officers very happy, as if they had planned an elaborate surprise party and the birthday boy had rewarded them with the classic, stunned, dumb look.

Some of us were hurt badly. A kid's arm was broken. A pregnant lady collapsed and had to be taken away a bit later. But most of us were simply hit hard across the back or arms and occasionally poked in the stomach in such a way as to be doubled up and left on the ground gasping for breath, the squirming target of short, swift kicks from a shoe tip. Being clubbed with a nightstick is easy to describe. A grown man holding a thick stick stands a few feet away from you. Now he hits you with that stick, hard, ten or twelve times—each time in a different place. Pain, yes, and panic also.

Though it seemed a chaotic melee to us, our group was actually being herded slowly away from the truck even as the beatings proceeded. We were in a grassy alley between two long, single-story, windowless, tin-roofed buildings. As the beatings continued, we were being edged down the alley toward an open door. By the time they had worked us the twenty yards to the door, the next truck was being backed into the alley with a whole new load of demonstrators about to get the surprise of their lives. We were, in fact, not at the city jail, but at the county fairgrounds on the outskirts of the city. I don't know how large the fairgrounds were, but they were fenced and gated, and the gate was guarded by police officers. We had been unloaded between two barns where livestock was exhibited at the annual fair. These barns would be our jail for the next days and weeks.

Once we'd been pushed and shoved through the sliding door into the barn, we were greeted by a scene of surreal serenity. It was as if what was happening outside was in a different world. Here, there were lots of city policemen, but no clubbing. They simply had us line up in a long single file. Halfway down the building there were ten card tables set up. At each one, a police clerk sat before a typewriter with stacks of paper on the floor on either side of him. Farther down the room, we saw a frightened, huddled group of women and young children who had already been processed.

When my turn came, I went to the desk and gave my name and age and address. Then I took my papers to a longer desk at the end, where I was fingerprinted and surrendered my papers. The women, girls, and children under six were sent to join the cluster across the room. We men and boys were directed out a door midway on the other side of the building.

I went through the door into the bright sunlight and the morning's second surprise. Another contingent of highway patrol officers was waiting there to give each new male guest an individualized greeting. There were about two dozen of them arranged in two parallel lines down the length of the building. I had to walk between the two rows of men with their clubs out. It was the classic gauntlet ordeal, but with local rules—no running. I had to walk it, and slowly. In the first chaotic group clubbing, it had been possible to protect myself somewhat. For one thing, there was so much confusion that, with a little luck, one might remain relatively unnoticed. Also, I had been able to shield myself somewhat from the blows with my arms. But out here it was different. I was the single target of the moment. When I raised my arms and ducked my head to block the club coming down from my right, the guy on the left whacked me on the thigh, slammed my lower back with his stick, or rapped me on my unprotected shins, or, worst of all, made a short sharp jab with the club's end into my ribs. I had the sense to keep walking, but all else in me turned stupid animal—that is, I responded instinctively to each poke and flat whack with a protective gesture and so was flailing back and forth between the two assault lines, always vulnerable, always twisting the wrong way at the wrong moment. It wasn't the physical pain that broke me—against that I had the protection of shock—but the humiliation of how vulnerable I was. By the time I got near the end of the line, the most sadistic officers were merely feinting a blow to rib or a gut jab—my own terror did the rest. I still feel the shame of those last ghost blows though the actual clubbing is long gone from my body memory.

At the end of the gauntlet, I staggered through another small door into an identical barn. In here, the other male prisoners were gathered in a loose group with armed guards all around them. We stood there for several hours while all the rest of the demonstrators were processed. If anyone tried to sit down on the concrete floor, guards came over with clubs and he scrambled to his feet again.

It became apparent that the processing was completed when more officers entered our building and began to form a circle around our loose cluster of about sixty men and teenage boys. The clubs were out again. There were probably about thirty officers loosely spaced in a ring ten feet back from our huddle. Gradually this ring tightened and our apprehensive cluster instinctively tightened too. Soon, we were jammed tighter together than we had been in the truck. The ring of officers was still about ten feet back from us, but now we could feel their menace though their manner was jocular. Suddenly, one or two officers would sprint across the bare space and deliver four or five fast blows to whichever unfortunates were there at the outer edge of our group.

Some of this clubbing now was different than earlier. For the first time, there was blood. I saw how surgical and calculated these blows were. A middle-aged white man with a dark beard seemed to have caught the attention of several officers. I saw two of them rush in and one swung his stick deftly toward the man's face. He wasn't trying to knock him unconscious (which he could easily have done). Instead, he hit him a glancing blow directly mid-forehead so the edge of the stick's end split the skin neatly and blood gushed down over his face. It probably hurt like hell, but the effect on the victim's neighbors was the real point of the technique. We were terrified to see his eyes staring out through a streaming mask of blood.

Not everyone clubbed at that time was bloodied, but the pattern was set. For the next half hour, there were sudden forays of assault meant to create complete panic, meant to make us turn against each other and fight and hurt each other in an effort to get near the center, away from the attacks. It didn't work. We certainly felt panic, but we held up pretty well and in fact, managed to move the littlest kids toward the center where they would be safe. Nobody tried to force his way to the middle.

During the Algerian war for independence, the French troops used the same technique on captured Algerians. It worked then, because they fired pistols into the packed cluster, killing those at the outer margin. Without that threat of death, it wasn't possible to get us to maim and smother each other as the Algerians had done in their panic.

It was now quite late in the afternoon and the clubbing had become perfunctory, desultory. Most of the eager brutalists had had their fill. Equally, on our side, the most insistently defiant had gotten their comeuppance, either by specially focused clubbing, or—for one or two of them—something really frightening: to be grabbed by two guards and dragged away. We never saw them again. They were probably taken to the city jail proper, but in those circumstances that was a terrible fate. A lot could happen to someone during a ride to the jail, and the isolation of individual cells was itself a danger. We knew we were far safer in a group together, no matter how nasty the guards felt.

Later that afternoon, we were told to line up in rows of ten about an arm's length apart. Then we sat down in place with our legs crossed loosely in front and our backs straight, as if we were Buddhist monks sitting in meditation. Now we were forbidden to so much as whisper. Guards moved back and forth among the rows, and if anyone put a hand on the ground, or leaned back on an arm or stretched, a guard would run up to kick him or threaten him with a club. This kept up for hours as the shadows deepened and at last the overhead lights came on, but they were small and distant and only made the floor where we sat seem darker and more shadowy.

Sitting on my right was a black kid, maybe ten or twelve years old. He was wearing one of the cheap Movement buttons on his shirt—"Freedom Now," it declared in bold black letters on a white background. One of the guards stopped in front of the kid, looked down at him and said: "Take off that damned pin, nigger." The kid quickly pulled it off—it was a simple open pin, nothing fancy like a safety pin.

"Put it in your mouth," he said. The kid opened his mouth and placed the pin on his tongue.

"Good. Now swallow it. Go ahead, damn you. I said swallow it."

I don't know how long it took him to say this. I was sitting on the floor only two or three feet from where the guard stared down at the terrified kid. I went crazy inside. All the fear and panic of the day reversed itself into pure rage. I felt it shooting up through me like a geyser. My personality, my passionately held pacifist beliefs were tossed aside like a toy plastic boat as the fountain of rage burst up. I wanted, with all my being, to kill that guard, to shoot him repeatedly with his own pistol, though I would as gladly and easily have strangled him with my bare hands. Within seconds, this over-whelming rage lost its shapelessness and became sharply honed—it focused on his pistol a scant two yards from me. But the pistol was held in its holster by a leather strap. Could I, with the element of surprise on my side, get the pistol loose and in my hands and shoot him enough times to kill him before the other guards pulled me off? That was the only question that concerned me. I needed to kill him, nothing but killing him would satisfy my rage. I sat there try-ing to calculate my chances and when to move, or even if I could move after having sat for painful hours in that awkward position. And of course, a part of me, separate from this blood rage, was ter-rified that I would be killed as well—that this homicidal act I yearned to commit would lead to my own death also.

All this was going on in seconds that were hours inside me, and all the while the kid sat there with the pin in his mouth. Had he so much as tried to swallow it, it would have stuck in his windpipe and he would have died, choking in horrible pain. "Swallow it," the guard said again and caressed his club. I'll never know if it was courage or the dumb luck of a throat too dry and constricted with fear, but the kid sat there without moving. I sat there, too, my common sense wrestling my rage to a standstill so all you could see was an intense trembling. And the guard stood there glaring down in the dark. At last, three of his fellow guards who until then had stood watching at a small distance, moved in and persuaded him to give it up.

I sat there in the quiet dark, while the adrenaline slowly ebbed from my veins. I was staring at the pile of rubble into which the whole moral architecture of my pacifist politics had collapsed. I had built everything on the solemn belief that I would never intentionally harm another human being. Since Peter's death, I'd felt the only way I could live with myself and permit myself to go on living was by renouncing all violent actions completely. I was convinced my pacifism was stable and sincere. (Hadn't I applied for conscientious objector status with my draft board?) But my homicidal rage in that barn showed me how little I knew myself and how different my ideals were from my emotional reality. I was not who I thought I was, or who I wanted to be. There were forces in me far stronger than my principles. My absolute and pure desire to kill that trooper exposed my pacifism as superficial, insincere, ridiculous. What else was down there inside me? What other large and powerful creatures lurked far beneath the tiny rowboat of my ego?

42

After the Long Day

THE LONG DAY WAS ALMOST OVER. IT TURNED OUT WE WERE sitting on the floor waiting for a truckload of mattresses to arrive. When they came, we unloaded them. At this point, to honor the fact that this cow barn had become a semi-official Mississippi jail, we prisoners were segregated by race. Whites were told to put their mattresses in rows in one part of the barn, blacks in another, with a space of twenty yards between.

We had no sheets, blankets, or pillows, but who cared? By then, we weren't expecting hotel accommodations. Our guards, too, were tired. Though they had taken off their sunglasses, they still wore the awkward helmets that covered their hair and ears; they still had their badges taped.

Exhausted and disoriented, we lay down on the moldy mattresses.

And that was the last we ever saw of our highway patrol hosts.

When we woke, shivering in the dawn chill, it was to face a whole new set of guards. These men weren't highway patrolmen at all. They wore the green and gray uniforms of the Fish and Game Service—they were game wardens! True, they still carried revolvers and had nightsticks stuck on their belts, but they were older, bare-headed and open-faced, with clearly numbered badges.

Around eight, we were ushered outside for breakfast. An outdoor kitchen had been set up between our barn and the women's barn next door. We picked up metal trays and stood in line to get a helping of grits, a scoop of syrup, and a piece of Wonder bread—all slopped down directly onto the tray. At the end of the line we took a spoon from a large heap. When we had finished eating, we got in another line where we were given a metal hook which we slipped through a hole in one corner of our tray. We then passed in front of two huge metal drums set up over gas burners—the first drum, on a low flame, was filled with soapy water; the second, under a high flame, simmered just below the boiling point. Holding the end of the hook, you dipped your tray first in the soapy water, then the hot rinse, then placed it back on the pile to be used at lunch.

The only violence of the morning happened there. It's hard to say if it was an accidental screw-up or malice—the kid may have misunderstood a guard's snarled order, or maybe he did as he was told. However it happened, he thrust his whole arm into the boiling water. We saw the guards lead him off, woozy and sick-faced with shock.

When we returned to our barn, we were feeling much better. By now, we realized that the worst was over—that the anonymous guards who could act with impunity were gone, perhaps for good, certainly for the moment. We even began singing songs to lift our spirits—"Keep Your Eyes on the Prize," "Ain't Gonna Study War No More," "We Shall Overcome." Through the two walls of cement block separating us, we could even hear the faint sound of the women singing across the way, and this cheered us to further and louder singing—as though with our voices we could bridge the gulf between our two groups and abolish the memory of the calamities that had befallen us since we'd come to this place.

Then, late in the morning, a city police official entered our barn and announced that the FBI had arrived and if anybody had complaints about how they had been treated, now was their opportunity to make their statements. There wasn't a prisoner there who hadn't been beaten and clubbed more than once, but only about twenty of us stepped forward. Maybe the most seasoned veterans knew better; maybe those local citizens who'd never been arrested before were afraid to draw more attention to themselves.

When my name was called, I was conducted outside and taken into the broad, grass-grown alley between the two barns where we were first unloaded from the trucks. At one end, five or six FBI agents had set up tables, typewriters, and chairs under a bright yellow canvas awning. I was shown a seat and the agent introduced himself and set a piece of paper into his typewriter. "Now, I understand you have something to say about how you have been treated. What happened and when? I need as many details as possible."

For the next half hour, I went over each instance of unprovoked violence. As I unfolded my narrative from our first arrival at that very spot where now we sat, a spot where the grass was still trampled and here and there spattered with yesterday's blood, the agent kept politely interrupting: "You say a man in a highway patrol uniform hit you over the back of your head with a club—could you give me a detailed description of that person?" "Can you give me the number of the officer's badge?" Well, of course not—that's what the tape was for. Only gradually did I begin to catch on. I could just as easily have stopped midway through my complaint, since I saw the absurdity of trying to connect my experiences with any identifiable perpetrator. I kept on, partly out of stubbornness, partly because it felt good to be outside. Partly because I thought the FBI agents were sincere, that they really were there to help me. I believed since they were federal agents and took their orders from Washington, they were untainted by the evil that was operating here at the state and local police levels. But, had they arrived any time during the preceding afternoon, there would have been no need for this complaint

I was so solemnly swearing to. They could have arrested the perpetrators in the very act. Slowly it dawned on me that it had all been prearranged between the Jackson authorities and the FBI. The FBI chose not to show up until late that morning—hours after the brutal, anonymous patrolmen had been replaced by their innocuous confreres, the game wardens. The media—that third partner in the dance between the Movement and the Southern authorities—had been completely outwitted. The fairgrounds were fenced off; the gate was guarded the whole time we were there. All the reporters and news cameras saw and reported was a well-mannered and restrained mass arrest on the sidewalks of Jackson.

Even now, feeling again that frustrated rage at the authorities and anger at my own naïveté as I relive that day, I want to shout: You see, it was all planned! The whole thing was planned by intelligent people with political authority. All that advance planning with the trucks, the escort, and the remote, guarded fairgrounds was the Big Wheel. Inside that encompassing wheel was the smaller wheel of the police violence. But even the Small Wheel was planned, not spontaneous. Planned the way a parent plans a child's birthday party: first we'll have a greeting of guests, then later we'll have a treasure hunt, and then, when they're all tired, we'll play pin-the-tail-on-the-donkey. Some midlevel police brass had sketched the day's activities out in such a way that his officers would have ample opportunity to express their feelings about us with their clubs. And the whole thing moved with awesome smoothness: "a wheel inside a wheel" like Ezekiel's vision. The efficiency with which the day's events unfolded was clear evidence of rational, intentional evil—a small-scale version of the orderly mindset that went into creating the Nazi camps.

And there at the center, at least for me, barely contained within the two wheels of bureaucratic violence, was the genuinely spontaneous, psychopathic evil of the guard who tried to make the kid swallow the pin. The outer wheels you can analyze and explain and graph and deplore. You can even, if you want to, expose them to the light of day and regulate them out of existence. But who can shine a light into that solitary soul and see anything but darkness?

Over the course of the next several days, routine established itself. Though our new guards might not have cared much for us, their idea of harassment was ludicrously mild—banging their clubs against the metal chairs at night to wake us up, abusive language, and an occasional shove. Mostly, they settled down to playing all-night poker. We were allowed to go to the bathroom once a day, standing in lines of twenty at a time to use the two toilets.

Word came in from outside that the Movement's plan was to try to make this demonstration a large and ongoing one to attract national attention. They hoped to get Martin Luther King Jr. to visit. Meanwhile, the most important thing was for as many of us as possible to stay in jail as long as possible. The city had offered to let anyone loose who would pay the $50 fine and admit guilt, but we were urged to hold on. It was hot and boring during the day, chilly at night. Each morning, the mattresses were stacked against a wall, so we had no comfortable place to sit for the rest of the day. There was no exercise of any kind—we couldn't even walk outside a chalked rectangle enclosing us without attracting a guard's atten-tion. We were fed grits, syrup, and a slice of bread for breakfast. Lunch and dinner were two vegetables, grits, and powdered milk so watered down you could see clear to the bottom of the twenty-gallon pot it came in. Clearly, the City of Jackson had no intention of going bankrupt buying vittles for criminals.

Miserable as this food was, and despite the fact that there was almost no protein, we all felt noticeably better after meals, and it became a ritual to sing when we got back from eating. That lasted until the first Sunday. It dawned. We got up and stretched, sat around talking, waiting for the breakfast summons. It never came. It turned out that Sunday was special. It was special in that we would be fed only two meals instead of the usual three. When we returned from lunch that day, no one sang. No one sang from there on in. We hung on, but we hung by a thread.

As the days went by, people got out. All you had to do was go up to a guard and say you wanted to make bail. The Movement had money there to cover anyone. They wanted us to stay in, but if we wanted out, they would pay our fine and we would be released. The youngest and oldest got out pretty quickly, but a core group settled in for the duration. I don't know how many women, but perhaps thirty guys decided to stick it out.

There wasn't much to do except talk, and even that took more energy than many of us had. With the amount of calories we were getting, calisthenics were out of the question. Conversations were forbidden across the space between blacks and whites.

I don't remember any specific conversations during those long eventless days, but I do know that in its own way that lull demoralized me as much as the police violence. My Northern colleagues and I had all made the same choice in coming to Mississippi: to act decisively for a cause we believed in. We had signed on for action. Marooned on the floor of the cattle barn, we were like so many starfish stranded on a beach while the tide was out. Only the tide never returned. A number of my colleagues had been in Mississippi for some time and they had friends and projects they could imagine getting back to, but I had only just arrived and had no personal connections to draw on for sustenance. All I knew of Mississippi was what the troopers taught me and what my fellow volunteers revealed in desultory conversations. The more I talked with my colleagues, the more uneasy I felt. I wasn't the only one who'd come south propelled as much by a secret psychology as by political idealism. There wasn't anything wrong with these personal motives, but it was a little startling to hear them emerge as we sat on the floor in the enforced, traumatized lassitude of those long, sweltering afternoons.

I felt defeated by the beatings and the realization of the official, calculated evil behind them, but I also felt defeated from within. I had come here so that action could simplify my life and quiet the demons inside me. But in jail I wasn't *doing* anything. I couldn't *do* anything. If you can't do, you must be. And being was unbearable to me because it meant sinking back into a jumble of guilt, shame, and rage.

I had known all along that I was a pawn in the game. But I was beginning to feel that even that was a self-important delusion. Being a pawn would have made me one of eight. The chessboard of even the most minor historical skirmish (like our now-forgotten demonstration in Jackson) is larger and more complex than that. In that game, I was one of my side's three hundred pawns. So many no one kept track of them, or could keep track of them. No one single mind and hand planned the moves. It was more as if the pawns wandered about partly on their own, yet the forces around them and the other pieces arrayed against them were vastly more powerful than they were. The pawn was a part of the game, but a laughable, impotent part unless it participated (half-willingly?) in a spectacular self-sacrifice like that of Goodman, Schwerner, and Chaney. They had risen in status from pawns to martyr-heroes. They had become Really Important Pawns (RIP), but as I sat on the barn floor in Jackson day after stinking day, rubbing the bruises clubs had left, I began to realize that RIP also meant "Rest in Peace" and was only achieved by the pawn's death. And now that I knew what it felt like to be beaten and threatened, I wasn't all that eager for this elevation in status that would call for my dying. My love of life began to assert itself.

Still, the days went by and I hung in there. Then, on the tenth day, a guard came in and called my name. I had a phone call, he announced. It was Dave Hendler, my father's lawyer from Hudson.

"Listen," he said, "I've talked to people in the DA's office down there, and all you have to do is walk. You're free. They don't want you."

I mumbled something or other in response.

"Let's be clear here," he said. "I don't give a flying fuck for you or your damned cronies, but your father is my friend and he's going crazy with worry. I told him I'd get you out of there and I will. I want you to promise me you'll get out of Mississippi and come back here right now."

Here was a guy who knew how to handle people—his bullying tone and mention of my father's misery was just the right combination to extract my promise. By now, I was scared, lonely, and confused, and I would never again have a clearer opportunity to return to a safe place. I gave my promise and hung up.

A policeman standing nearby seemed to already know the upshot of my call and told me to follow him to his car. I was demoralized by my conversation with Hendler and ashamed of capitulating. I was also deeply overwhelmed by all I'd been through—the beatings, the apparent connivance of the FBI, my own murderous rage, and the confusing conversations I'd had with my fellow volunteers. The policeman dropped me off where I'd left my car in a vacant lot in the black section of Jackson. I got in and started driving. I should have stopped at SNCC headquarters and told them I was leaving, but I didn't. I should have said something about the route I was taking, an elementary safety precaution. I was simply ashamed to be deserting my post.

Still, I was so glad to be free. I hadn't bathed or changed my clothes in ten stinking-hot days. I put on a clean shirt from my suitcase in the trunk, but other than that I had no intention of stopping for even the most basic grooming until I felt safe. And to feel safe I had to put as much distance between myself and Jackson, Mississippi, as I possibly could.

43

Hayneville

ONCE I'D DECIDED TO LEAVE THE SOUTH, I COULDN'T GET OUT fast enough. From Jackson, I had several possible routes. I decided to head directly for Montgomery, Alabama. There, I could pick up the interstate (which was far safer) and I'd be retracing my route down, which would also feel reassuring. Still, the journey from Jackson to Montgomery was only by state routes and the last fifty miles of it was the stretch of State Route 80 between Selma and Montgomery where only three months before the famous march had taken place.

The journey out of Mississippi was uneventful and once I'd crossed the state line, my spirits picked up. To celebrate my "escape" I put on the wide-brimmed, straw "planter's" hat I'd bought earlier in Mississippi. Such hats were functional against sun glare in the fields, but they were also part of an informal uniform for rural civil rights volunteers. Wearing it, I felt I better resembled the competent, effective activist I longed to be. But I was only fooling myself as I fled north. If we were soldiers, then I was a deserter, but one without the sense to change his uniform for civilian clothes as he fled the front lines.

I passed through Selma around dinner time, but didn't stop. I wanted to get at least as far as Montgomery before I paused. I was about fifteen miles beyond Selma, out in farm land, when I heard a police siren behind me. I wasn't speeding, that was certain. Looking in my rearview mirror, I saw that the car behind me was simply a fairly new white Chevy, not a patrol car. But it was flashing its lights and it was clearly the source of the siren. I decided it must be an unmarked police car and pulled over onto the shoulder with the white car right behind me.

As soon as I'd stopped, two men jumped out of their car and ran up on either side of my own. One was a chunky guy with a florid face; the other was lean and taller. They both had thick black pistol belts and had drawn their revolvers. And yet they wore civilian clothes—no uniforms, no badges, just the drawn pistols pointed toward me.

This was exactly what every Movement worker dreaded—an ambush. That mine was taking place at dusk on a state highway, with cars passing every few minutes or so, didn't make any difference. And weren't we on the same stretch of highway where only a few months before a car had pulled alongside Mrs. Liuzzo late at night as she ferried marchers from Selma? Hadn't someone in that car rolled down the window and fired a shotgun point-blank into her face? I sat there behind my steering wheel with the armed men on either side of my car.

What could I do? As I'd seen them climb out with their guns, I'd rolled up my windows and locked the doors, but what did that accomplish? Cartoon of the goldfish in a bowl, the leering cat tapping its claws against the glass wall. The one guy on my side rapping his pistol barrel on the window glass inches from my face, then pointing it straight at me.

"Get out, you little son of a bitch."

"Who are you, kid? What the fuck are you doing here?"

"I was visiting my brother in the Air Force in Biloxi."

"Shit, you must think we're pretty dumb. Where'd you get that hat?"

"I bought it."

"What have you got in this car of yours? Why don't you just open the trunk and let us look?"

I was scared now. This was serious trouble. I stood with my back against the side of my car and my hands in the air. The one who was asking most of the questions kept jabbing his pistol into my stomach for punctuation. In the gray twilight, cars passed with their headlights on like willfully innocent goggle eyes that refused to blink or focus on the drama being enacted on the road's shoulder.

As the chubby one held me at gunpoint, the other searched my trunk and quickly found Movement pamphlets.

"Eureka! We got him! We got the son of a bitch!"

I'd learn later that, to them, I was a civil rights organizer who was rumored to be headed toward their town of Hayneville. Hayneville, a tiny hamlet fifteen miles off the highway in the middle of the swamps, county seat of Lowndes County, 80 percent black and one of the fiercest bastions of racism in the state. But these two guys had staked out this highway; they were going to get that bastard before he got to their town. And what were they going to do with me, now that they had me? Well, they were going to take care of me just the same way that lady from Detroit had been taken care of a few months back. I would see what happened to people who messed with their town:

"Son, we're going to dump you in the swamp."

One of them put my wallet in his shirt pocket.

"You get in your damned car, and you follow us, boy." Having scurried back to their own vehicle, they pulled out onto the highway in front of me. I pulled out, too, and began to follow them. It was dark now, the whole scene had barely taken ten minutes. What did I know? That they had guns; that they said they were cops but had never offered proof of any sort, unless you counted the siren hidden in their car grill. They said they were going to kill me and leave me in the swamps; they also said that I was going to come with them and be put in jail. They had my wallet, but I was alone in my car as we moved down the highway at about forty miles an hour.

Suddenly, they signaled a right turn onto a narrow, unmarked road. What now? What should I do? Where did this road go? I had only seconds to decide what to do. My car was a good six years older than theirs and nowhere near as fast. If I kept going down Route 80 as fast as I could go, they could quickly overtake me and then what? They had the guns, they had my wallet—they could shoot me, they *would* shoot me—I had been resisting arrest! All this in seconds in my mind and I made my choice and turned off onto the small road.

Already the white car was speeding away from me, as if I were pursuing it. The road we were on now was a thin, twisting ribbon of asphalt. I never saw a single light from a house anywhere along it, nor did we pass a single other car. I had to speed as fast as I dared to try to keep up with them. But why? Why was I trying to stay up? In my headlights, I could see the steep shoulderless road yielding to thick trees on either side—we really were going into the swamps! I was racing toward my own murder, trying hard to stay up with my murderers as if they were my kindly guides without whom I would be hopelessly lost in a dark forest. This was genuine madness. Not the split-second madness of deciding whether or not to turn off Route 80, but an excruciating insanity that stretched itself out over whole minutes at a time. And the same simple thoughts screamed through my head again and again: "They are going to kill you, just like they promised they would! And you are driving fast to your own funeral, which is insane!" "OK, what do I do, then? Do you want me to turn around? How? How can I turn around on this road in the dark? Do you want me to screech to a stop at the widest part or at some place where a road goes off (if there ever is one and I see it as I race past)? And if I do, if I do manage to turn around and make a run for it—what chance will I have on this road I don't know and them with guns?" "OK, asshole, don't make a run for it— instead drive on like this, right to your own death. Become the stu- pidest death in the entire history of the Civil Rights Movement —the jerk who drove to his own graveside and thereby obligingly disposed of the evidence his car might provide." "What do I care about evidence! I just don't want to die! What am I supposed to do?"

My brain screamed back and forth at itself as my body raced along through the dark trying to keep their taillights in sight, my knuckles white as bone, clutching the steering wheel. Those moments of horror in that car are as absolute as what I felt the day of Peter's death. Horror and panic and pure vulnerability.

How long did this nightmare go on? I can show you, I can show myself the road that leads in a meandering, lazy way through the swamps from Route 80 to Hayneville—it's maybe ten miles. Let's say it was twenty minutes before I saw the houses and shacks of Hayneville, before we passed the dark courthouse set back on its green lawn and pulled into the driveway to park behind the two- story cinder-block building that was the county jail. Twenty min- utes. But that drive is outside all time for me. It's not a time but a place—a place seared into my brain and when I go to that place, as I have now to retell it, the clock stops entirely and I'm trapped inside the screaming, silent terror again.

I felt an almost ludicrous relief as their car pulled to a stop beside the jail and I pulled in behind them. It was almost with joy that I confronted the uniformed sheriff as his "special unpaid deputies" turned me over to his rightful authority. I felt safe and grateful to be taken upstairs and placed in my own small cell.

The next morning an old black man brought me some breakfast, the first food I'd seen since the previous morning at the jail in Jackson. The guy who brought my tray was a trusty, a prisoner who did chores around the jail in exchange for being let out of his cell. He told me a few things about my situation: "Sometimes the sheriff beats them, sometimes he doesn't." It didn't seem clear to him yet which category I would fall into, but the possibility of a beating didn't scare me in the least. My experience last evening on the highway and during the long drive there had given me the gift of perspective. I was alive. It was good to be alive. My chances of staying alive were considerably better than they had seemed only a few hours ago.

But my chances of being happily alive depended in part on what I ate. This generous country breakfast—a feast after the stingy rations in Jackson—was a secret threat to my well-being. The syrup was richer, the heap of grits huge, and there was a small stack of fat-back, too—deep-fried pork rinds. The grease in the fatback was my undoing. I gobbled everything down and then, an hour later, was doubled over with horrible cramps and spent the morning puking into the lidless toilet that abutted my metal bunk.

I'd been placed in the farthest cell of a small wing on the second floor. It was about four feet by eight feet, with nothing in it but a metal bunk like a shelf bolted to the wall and a toilet in the corner. If I shimmied up the bars, I could just glimpse some tree branches out a small, high window on the corridor wall. I was the only prisoner in that part of the jail. In fact, except for the trusty, I never saw or spoke to anyone else for the entire eight days I spent there. Ultimately, that amounted to solitary confinement, but it could have meant something worse. If no other prisoners saw me at the jail, it would mean that many fewer witnesses if they did make up their minds to do me some real harm or even make me vanish. My isolated cell may have been a sign that they hadn't yet decided what to do with me. On top of that, there was the major fact that no one on earth except my captors had any idea of where I was. All my father's lawyer knew was that I had promised to head north. No one else knew anything of my whereabouts and so no one would be looking for me when I failed to arrive somewhere.

Still, things could have been worse. The whole first day went by without my being beaten by the sheriff. Nor did I see any more of the two characters who had terrorized me on the highway.

On the third day, the sheriff and I had a little talk. He said he'd been in touch with state authorities in Montgomery and that I was going to have a visitor. That afternoon, I was escorted the half block to the county courthouse where I met a man in a gray suit who looked a bit like an FBI agent. He was an investigator for the Department of Public Safety. He explained to me that he was part of a unit that had been set up to help the FBI investigate links between the Civil Rights Movement and communists. He wanted to ask me some questions.

We sat at a small table in a room and he gathered as much information as he could about me, my family and siblings, and any organizations I might belong to. It was really pretty straightforward. I don't think he ever bothered to ask if I was a communist or anything that unsubtle. But he seemed to feel that this information, added to other data they were accumulating, would be of real interest to someone someday. He thanked me and we parted—he back to Montgomery, me to my cell.

In the whole story of my imprisonment in Hayneville, that investigator might count as an angel who inadvertently saved me. Three or four days after I'd left Jackson, Dad began to worry about what had happened to me. The indefatigable Hendler set to work again tracking me down. His phone call to the state attorney general's office in Montgomery brought some news. The attorney general at the time was a man named Flowers. He had ambitions to be governor himself, and part of his strategy was to present himself as a racial moderate in a state known for its appallingly racist state officials. So, a call to Flowers's office fell on attentive if not necessarily sympathetic ears. Yes, as a matter of fact, they had heard of me. I was being held in Hayneville down in Lowndes County; their office had sent an investigator down there only the other day to interview me. No, they couldn't help more than to give that information. Lowndes County was a hellhole; they made their own laws down there. No one from Montgomery was about to go messing around with those folks.

So, the news Dave Hendler gleaned from Montgomery was both reassuring—they had located me—and alarming: Hayneville was not a safe place. It played by its own rules and they were very violent, a fact Mrs. Liuzzo's death had already shown and the subsequent acquittal of her murderers in the Hayneville courthouse would confirm even further. I was to learn later that my father began concocting his own melodramatic plans at this point: he would fly to Montgomery with his pistol, rent a car, and come down and free me by force if necessary.

Fortunately, Hendler suggested a phone call direct to the Hayneville jail instead. When they reached the jail, it seemed that the sheriff couldn't let them talk to the prisoner and he couldn't come to the phone himself:

"No, I'm sorry. Why right now he's upstairs playing checkers with the boy. Don't you worry. He's having a fine time. He's just got to learn to slow down on the highway."

Of course, there wasn't a bit of truth in the checkers story. I imagine it was the sheriff himself they spoke to, and I must say he handled those Northerners rather cleverly. Still, it was now widely and definitively known that I was in jail in Hayneville. Even if my father and Hendler (both now angry at me for having gotten them so worried when I was really fine) ceased worrying for the moment about my situation, there would eventually be the question of how long I could be held there without any charges beyond the spurious one of speeding. From that point on, my release was only a matter of time.

Not that I knew that, or had any such encouraging sense of things. I knew nothing about anything. All I knew was that the days went by and I was left alone hour after hour and day after day, speaking with no one and with no clue as to my ultimate fate. I will say this: the sheriff let the trusty bring me two books from my car to read, E. M. Forster's *Aspects of the Novel* and a paperback text anthology of Romantic and Victorian English poetry (which I still have). I must have read the Forster book, but I don't remember anything about it, and whenever I see a vintage copy of that book with the same cover design as mine had, I feel slightly nauseated and angry. Likewise, I also developed an intense dislike of most Victorian poets, especially Matthew Arnold and George Meredith. On the other hand, my love for the Romantics, especially Keats and Wordsworth, deepened immeasurably. I read Wordsworth with pleasure because he seemed in touch with the actual, physical delights of nature. In Keats's poems, I felt the enormous inner turmoil and despair which were muffled in Wordsworth. I particularly loved Keats's nightingale ode and had no difficulty at all identifying with his desire to transcend bodily suffering through the ecstatic release imagination offered.

Still, it would be an error to give the impression that poetry was sustaining me in a steady way. I had been in jail at the fairgrounds for ten days in Jackson. Abruptly released from that experience, I had been arrested and terrorized again in Alabama on the very same day of my release from Jackson. And now I was back in jail, in solitary, with no one to talk to and no inkling as to my ultimate fate. I was, without quite realizing it, in very bad mental and emotional shape.

And the days went by. Probably the phone call to the sheriff set things moving toward my release, but they moved slowly. Ultimately, I would spend eight days in the Hayneville jail, but that number doesn't touch the feeling because the number presents a comprehensible limit. What I *felt* was each day stretching into the next with no information about anything. I didn't know that the sixth day was only a day or so from my release; that the seventh day, I had only to hold on for another twenty-four hours. To me, each of those days was its own excruciatingly long and anxious self;

for all I knew, it led only to another just like it. In short, I had lost hope. I no longer had a rational sense of my prospects, but where would I get such a sense? I still didn't know that anyone knew I was there.

And then, on the morning of the eighth day, the sheriff showed up at my cell with the keys and a big grin. Where were we going?

"Never you mind, sonny boy."

We were going to the courthouse again. This time, we entered a room filled with file cabinets and an old oak desk. The sheriff took down a huge ledger and opened it to a page where names and dates were written. I was free, the sheriff announced, as soon as I had signed myself out "under my own recognizance" as the legal term goes. All I had to do was put my signature and the date in the ledger, just below the names of others who had similarly signed themselves out.

I still had one unsettling surprise before I was free. The name immediately before the blank where I was to sign was also "ORR." What was this, I demanded to know? Was this some kind of trick? No, the sheriff assured me. The last prisoner to sign out had been named Orr too—a car thief headed for the state pen, whom they had put up for a few weeks. It was a coincidence that startled us both.

"You're free to go now. If you want my advice, you'll get your ass out of town as quick as you can." I hardly needed convincing. My Ford started up right away—that had been the last miracle I was praying for.

I drove out of Hayneville and I didn't stop. I didn't stop in Montgomery or anywhere else, except for gas. I drove night and day. I remember almost nothing of the drive except some surreal, shaky-handed struggle to shave and wash up at a rest stop on the interstate in the middle of the night. And another moment from the early hours of the morning as I drove up the New Jersey Turnpike. By then, I was so exhausted that I began to hallucinate huge, dog-sized rats scurrying across the lanes in front of me as I drove through the Hackensack marshes.

And then it was morning and I was back in Germantown. Safe and sound, as the expression goes. Safe and sound.

44

Safe and Sound

WELL, CERTAINLY SAFE, BY COMPARISON TO MY CIRCUMSTANCES
of only a few days before. But the notion of "sound" was more
problematic. I was exhausted. I was malnourished. Although I was
five feet eleven and had always been skinny, I now weighed only
110 pounds. These were problems that could be solved simply
enough. I slept. I ate. I slept again. Gradually my health returned.
My emotional recovery was another matter.

About a week and a half after I got back, I felt a wave of intense claus-
trophobia. I needed more air and space than I could get where I was.
I drove in my Ford out to the tip of Cape Cod, to the dunes near
Provincetown. I'd never been there before, but the fact that I had the
power to go to a place where land ended and the ocean began seemed
important. After the cramped terror of the Hayneville jail, I needed
the reassurance that I was really free—that I could, simply by deciding to do it, move spontaneously here or there. It was night when I
arrived. I parked my car along the edge of Route 6, climbed into the
back seat and slept. The next morning I hiked up and over the high,

roadside dunes and through several flat sand valleys to the beach. I lay down in the sun in my jeans and shirt. It was a cool morning and now the sun had burned off the mist. In the whole dome of the sky there wasn't a single cloud. I felt I was inside God's blue eye, an eye that had blinked itself clear of fogs and mysteries. I listened to the waves' irregular pulse. I was a dead thing washed up on the shore, the single speck lodged in God's pupil, but harmlessly, so small I could be absorbed. All was elemental now, unillusioned. I was safe. I sobbed for a while, but I'd never felt more blissful and empty.

Back in Germantown again, among normal people and circumstances, I was beginning to realize that something was wrong with me. I couldn't talk clearly, no matter what the subject. When I first got back, I tried to share some of my experiences with Jon, but what I had been through was so odd and confusing to me and so weighted down with emotions of terror and despair that I soon stopped trying to speak of it. But then I realized that no matter what the subject, I was no longer able to communicate normally. If I started to say something to someone—anything more complicated than "pass the salt"—I would become confused and lose my train of thought. Rather than stop once I saw I had forgotten what it was I was trying to say, I just kept talking on in an aimless, wandering way, all the time watching helplessly as my interlocutor's eyes and face gradually registered increasing uneasiness and even alarm. I myself was frightened in a numb way. I knew that my speech had somehow become a meandering babble of disconnected phrases, but once I'd begun to speak I couldn't stop. Each time I spoke I hoped I would sound normal. Each time, as I began to lose my focus, I clung to a vague sense that if I kept talking, I might somehow regain my meaning. I felt like someone being tested for sobriety with one of those video screens where a highway outline moves toward the little yellow car he is steering. In my case, the car would lurch off the highway in one direction and crash through a billboard but keep going as I struggled to regain the road, only to crisscross and slide off the other side, plowing through shrubbery and trees, and all the while the car hurtling forward and the landscape unrolling relentlessly toward me. Finally, whole excruciating minutes into my monologue, I would let go the wheel entirely and begin to repeat the phrase "I don't know, I don't know . . . " three or four times in an apologetic voice that trailed off into silence.

Now the ordinary language of conversation and communication seemed hopelessly beyond me and for the first time I was frightened by my isolation. Language and my own mind had betrayed me. I saw myself trying to throw out a rope of words toward my listener, as if I were a small boat in distress and they were a larger boat that had pulled alongside to help. But what the other person experienced was not a launch stalled in the water, but someone tossing limp noodles of spaghetti in all directions, like a demented toddler in a highchair.

If I thought I had left the hostility behind in the South, I was mistaken. My relationship with Inga had been such that for several years we never spoke to each other if it was possible not to. She made her feelings clear with a single pronouncement on the day I got back: "You got exactly what you deserved." I had expected no sympathy from her, but other responses caught me off guard.

I had lived in Germantown my whole life. I was the doctor's son—everyone knew me and I knew everyone. If you paraded them before me one at a time, I could have told you the names of half a thousand people who lived in our town and its surroundings. True, once I'd left for college I didn't come back, even for Christmas vacation, but all the more reason townsfolk might want to say something, at least "Hello. How are you?"

In fact, almost no one in Germantown would speak to me. It

was as if I weren't there, as if they passed a ghost or invisible person on the sidewalk. Given how difficult talking had become for me, I partly welcomed this silence, but if I was tempted to imagine this community silence as a sign of hushed concern around a convalescent, two incidents showed me otherwise. The first took place in Lawlor's. Once I realized what bad shape I was in, I began to regress in numerous ways, hoping I might find some healing in these retreats. And so I was sitting at the soda fountain in Lawlor's one day, sipping a Coke and leafing through a magazine, when a man who was the father of a high-school classmate of mine and a deacon in the Dutch Reformed Church I had sporadically attended as a kid came in to get his daily newspaper. Standing right next to me, he announced in a loud, steady voice: "Niggers are animals. They should shoot them all." Then he turned and walked out.

The only other person I remember speaking to me that summer was Mrs. Fraleigh, a second-grade teacher who must have been almost sixty then. One afternoon as I was emerging from Lawlor's, she crossed the street, walked right up to me and stood in such a way that I had to stop. "I don't care what they say, you did the right thing," she announced, then turned and walked away, leaving me staring dumbly into space.

When, later that summer, I got a chance to move to New York City and work for a small film company, I took it. I thought it might bring me out of my confusion and depression. I was wrong. The offer involved staying with the filmmaker and his family in their West Side apartment while I learned how to synchronize film and do elementary editing. Soon after I moved there, my boss, having taught me the rudiments, left with his family for the country. Staying alone for weeks in the apartment and working alone all day in a dark room in the office, I slipped deeper into a confused isolation.

I had gone south with the fervent, vague dream that I could

somehow redeem my misery through action in harmony with history and justice. I had thought that if I was lucky in a small way, I could lose my self-consciousness by working with others. If I was lucky in a big way, I might become a martyr for the cause. I dreamed of dying out of my tormented and confused life and rising up as other Movement martyrs had as an idealized face gracing a placard, a battle flag around which fellow idealists would rally.

My quests both large and small, had failed. I'd found I lacked the social skills for political work, and the Movement itself no longer had a clear idea of how to use its volunteers. As for my more exalted ambition, no matter how much I might long for the final stage when I was nothing but a poster and a martyr's name to be invoked in speeches or chanted in slogans, I had discovered I had no real taste for being beaten and brutalized.

Besides, I knew more about the world now. The car thief lying in the street, shot dead before my very eyes—hadn't he been resurrected the same way my civil rights martyrs had on the Atlantic City placards? Half a million people gazed at the image of his sprawled body filling the whole front page of the *Daily News* as they drank their morning coffee or hung from a strap in the lurching subway.

But this body that half a million people absorbed? One day, it was a person running in the street. That same day: a lifeless corpse. The next day, a picture in a newspaper. Later that same day, nothing but the trash that fills the mesh baskets on street corners or blows down windy alleys.

When the thief died, he was simply dead. When the news photo reduced him from three dimensions to two, it didn't invest him with higher meanings. The photo only made the meaninglessness of his existence multiple, spread its pointlessness across five hundred thousand identical pages.

When I read about Lester Smallman killing the seminary student on the same Hayneville streets where I had walked a few weeks before, I felt how close I had actually come to the death I had half courted. Oddly enough, it was Smallman, the murderer, whose face was immortalized in the *Times*—there was no picture of his victim. In fact, the whole article was about Smallman—his history and opinions, the fact that he spoke "not in the whining tone of the rural white working class but in the mellow, cultivated accent of the 'old family' Southern white." The newspaper was fascinated by Smallman, not the young man he'd murdered. I might have lost my only life in that backwater Alabama town, and in the process succeeded only in elevating my murderer to momentary celebrity.

I understood some things now, but also felt I understood nothing. I stood on the window ledge high above the street trying to get everything clear, trying to understand the emotional confusion inside me. But I couldn't. Instead, I just held on. And holding on, I made it through the summer.

45

The Other Field

AT THE END OF SUMMER, THE WEEK BEFORE I WAS
due back at school, I accepted an invitation from Mrs. Irving, my
former English teacher, to visit her for a day in Keene Valley in the
Adirondacks where she had a trailer on a small piece of land.

I don't know what we spoke about. I don't even know whether
I was speaking then, speaking coherently. I know that I no longer
made any effort to tell people my experiences. It had to do with a
sense of vulnerability that terrified me and that I couldn't share with
anyone.

But she didn't expect me to talk. The minute I pulled into her
driveway, she said: "Get back in your car, I want to show you something."

As I drove south, following her instructions to the nearby village of Bolton's Landing, she told me about the sculptor David
Smith, who had lived there. He had been killed just that spring
when his pickup truck crashed as he was returning from teaching at
Bennington College. I didn't know his work; I'd never heard of
him. We stopped at a diner and got directions to his place.

Because of some legal confusion about Smith's estate, every-thing had been left exactly as it was at his death. When we found his place at last—way up a dirt road—we saw a nondescript, cinder-block house set back against pines on the far side of a rectangular, low-mown meadow. The meadow sloped gently a hundred yards down a hill to end in woods. Near the road where we parked was a large shed flanked by rusting piles of metal and welding rods. Large, flat slabs of steel leaned against its outer wall. This was David Smith's workshop, which he had called the Terminal Iron Works. But it was the field itself that was amazing. Smith had filled it with his sculptures, arraying almost three hundred of them in long rows across the field.

Ignoring the "No Trespassing" signs nailed to the roadside trees, we climbed through the barbed-wire fence. Easy enough for me. I'd been crossing such fences all my life, but it was a struggle for Mrs. Irving, who was very stout.

When we stood at the edge of the field, she looked at me with a little smile and said, "Amazing, isn't it?" Then she turned and walked off among the metal figures. For the next hour, we each of us made our own way among the pieces, gazing at them and listen-ing to our own thoughts and responses. Smith's figures consisted of welded shapes of rusting industrial-red steel, or stacked moons and triangles of brushed aluminum welded in an almost infinite variety of intersecting planes and forms. Each piece was taller than a person and organized on a vertical axis, and though they were abstract and endlessly inventive in their shapes and textures and styles, you had a sense that they all made some urgent if obscure reference to the human figure.

Some of the pieces were raw iron spattered with rust from being left open to the elements. Rust, but not blood. These bodies didn't bleed. They had risen as if out of the soil itself like the dragon's teeth Cadmus sowed in the ancient Greek myth that came up as armed soldiers and fought each other to death. But these statues were soldiers of art. They brought no mayhem—only a longing to rise up and stand inside meaning as a man might stand in armor. There would be no violent struggles here. This was a field of blessing. A field where the mortal and fallen rose up, transformed.

I had made a long journey South to join the army of history. Here in this field, arrayed in long lines, was an army of art. This army was engaged in a war against the nothingness and indifference of the universe. It wasn't the kind of war history fought, where timing was everything and the clocks ran on blood. This was a war outside time. It was a war where you didn't fight, or march, or do violence to anyone.

Against the surrounding chaos and the desolate feel of the dead sculptor's house and padlocked forge, each welded presence seemed to say: this is art's way of fighting—to stand very still. This is art's way of fighting—not to do battle, but to concentrate emphatic being in an object.

These figures had stepped outside time in their heavy armor. No, they *were* their armor. They were armor animated, alive. Alive with the certainties and power of geometric shapes—the calm completeness of circles, the thrust of vectors shooting off at odd angles, the urgencies and contradictions of steel beams meeting and crossing. But always, or almost always, there was the ghost of a human figure in their vertical axis and scale. It was as if these figures dramatized different states of their maker's consciousness, different possibilities latent in him that had been given forceful and autonomous form. Smith's army was made up of figures whose fight was internal; you could see their energy zooming back and forth in the geometry of planes and angles. The forces were within them, in intense interaction, yet each figure retained its upright shape, its dignity as of a standing, unafraid individual. Somewhere in this field was a rendering in iron or steel of each agony and exultation Smith had ever felt. And I could feel them, too. I knew that somewhere in this field Cain stood; somewhere else, his slain brother.

There in that field of David Smith's figures, I saw what I could do. The martyr's cross I'd lugged the six years since Peter's death—I saw it now alchemized and shining, metamorphosed before my eyes into a hundred expressive shapes. And each shape said: "Let's live. Let's endure. Let us even exult that we have survived." Here was my blessing. Not with a blowtorch and sheet metal, but with pen and pencil. With a page and what words could conjure on it.

It was as if I had been standing in an earlier field for six long years, a field that had only a single, dead center: the place where Peter's body lay and where time had stopped and nothing moved, not even the wind. David Smith's field was different: No ghost haunted it, as Peter's ghost haunted the other. In Smith's field, the story was peacefully resolved. It was a field of life and of art. The figures were still, but they did not stop time in the way that Peter's corpse stopped time for me—time was not shocked into stasis by Smith's figures. Time moved around their stillness: the clouds and the seasons passed over the field, the rain fell, the stars looked down. Here was meaning in the midst of time's flowing. Here was the human spirit rising up, trying to transcend the limitations of our mortal, human bodies and at the same time celebrate them. Trying to transcend time, and yet also yielding to it, letting rust happen, letting the colors fade in the sun. Rust was not blood. These sculptures were alive and yet would not die. The sculptor was dead. But what he had created moved on beyond him, proclaiming some powerful, mysterious significance.

It all made sense to me there in the field as I wandered among the metal figures. This was the world of wonder that could come out of a single person's imagination. These were the meanings and celebrations of the will to live, of the passion to dramatize what it meant to be alive. There in the field I understood what I had been searching for.

I could choose to break the image of death that took me to Mississippi. I could choose instead the artist's kind of death that is part of being reborn a hundredfold. I had gone south to die, but I didn't. I had died in some way, though, some important way that is related to the dream of being reborn as language or, as Smith had been, into figures of metal. I wanted to be born again as something deathless and secular—like his statues that stood out there in the field in all weathers. Under the stars and through the long winters when the snow bandaged the ground. And in the summers when the clouds slid over and were gone—swift as thoughts that darken your brow and then pass. And the wind: moving through them and across them—flowing like water, like the Renssalaerville Falls flowing over the rocks that gleamed in the light.

To make poems like the statues that stood up so bravely in David Smith's field next to the Terminal Iron Works. They were in the universe, but different from it. Man made them. He was saying something when he did so. These statues speak the language of being. They whisper the story of life. Life and more life. Going on; the ongoing. The person who made them has perished, has joined the ocean of oblivion and moves with its currents, as does my father, my brother, my mother, Charley Hayes. As I will some day. Against that oblivion, there is this standing up, this lifting in a gesture of acknowledgment toward the sky and the earth and all that is around us.

And time moves through the statues and over them as sun and rain and cloud-shadow. Look, the clouds move over the field, over the statues with their open faces and upraised visages. They consider the sky: how it is blue and empty. How beautiful it is.